THE PERFECT SQUELCH

The Curtis Publishing Company
Indianapolis, Indiana

THE PERFECT SQUELCH

Last Laughs and Caustic Comments from
THE SATURDAY EVENING POST

The Perfect Squelch
President, The Curtis Book Division: Jack Merritt
Managing Editor: Jacquelyn S. Sibert
Designer: Pamela G. Starkey
Assistant Editor: Amy L. Clark
Editorial Assistant: Melinda A. Dunlevy
Compositors: Patricia Stricker, Penny Allison, Kathy Simpson
Technical Director: Greg Vanzo

Contents

Jest Plain Folks   1

No Place Like Home   25

Word War III   37

All Kidding Aside   57

Beat the Clock   67

Starcastic Remarks   95

Jest Plain Folks

Fashion Plate

Among the Baltimore men who dined together regularly at the Maryland Club was a big and not altogether modest fellow with a pronounced liking for conspicuous clothes. His checks, plaids and other sartorial glories constantly tried the eyesight of his beholders, but he spared them nothing.

One spring day he swept into the club clad in a new and notably colorful outfit. After marching the length of the lounge, he sat down in a chair from which he could see and be seen. To his gratification, his new clothes attracted a number of comments. He was stung, however, when one of his oldest friends gave him one glance and remarked, "Humph! Some outfit."

Slapping himself on the chest, the radiant chap boomed, "Take a good look, Ewing! It takes a real man to wear clothes like these!"

"Well," replied his friend, "you should have thought of that before you bought them."

—Frank R. Kent

Out of Control

Each time the timid-looking man began testifying at his hearing on a traffic accident, his wife interrupted to give her version. The judge listened impatiently as she corrected and reviewed all the facts. Finally the husband was asked, "Did you have complete control of your car at the time of the accident?"

Before the wife could speak up, the judge rapped his gavel.

"Unnecessary question," he said with a glance of understanding at the timorous defendant. "Testimony has already been given that at the time the accident occurred this man was accompanied by his wife."

—*Lois Carlon*

Smack

Janice was a meddler and worse. One of three sisters, she constantly embarrassed the two others with their boy friends. She cloaked her spite and jealousy with smiles, but made life miserable by her eavesdropping and tale-bearing.

One Sunday afternoon, she intercepted the boy that her older sister had been out with the night before. Pursing her lips in a simulated kiss, she made a smacking sound and asked: "What was that noise I heard as you said good night to Doris?"

The young man, momentarily embarrassed, soon recovered.

"That?" he said. "It seemed to come from the other room. Was it your ear pulling away from the wall?"

—*Mrs. A.G. Korelva*

Jest Plain Folks

"Number, please. . . ."

Although Granny is getting up in years, there's absolutely nothing wrong with her eyesight. But she dislikes using the telephone directory. Whenever she desires to phone a friend whose number she can't recall offhand—and this happens more and more frequently—she dials information instead of looking in the telephone book.

The "Voice With the Smile" requests her, of course, to make use of the directory. Whereupon Granny states very plaintively that her sight is failing and that she has just broken her glasses. Actually, she hasn't any to break. When we shake our heads reprovingly at Granny's duplicity, she scornfully mutters something about not having time to be bothered with looking up phone numbers.

A few days later the usual byplay with the operator took place. Granny, smiling in triumph to let us know that her system was the one for getting things done, dialed the number given her.

"Hello," she said, quite pleased with herself.

"Good morning," came the prompt reply. "Wills Eye Hospital. . . ."

—James Augustyn

3

Heard A Beef

cobean

The streetcars in Indianapolis were long past their prime 35 years ago, but somehow they managed to keep going. What they lacked in smoothness and accommodations, the motormen and conductors conscientiously tried to make up by giving extra service to their customers.

One morning Bill, one of the best-liked motormen on the line, happened to be piloting an exceptionally old, dilapidated car. It banged and rattled and grated to a stop at every intersection. In a select residential district, an overmatronly lady with the air of one who would use a streetcar only as a grim last resort beckoned to Bill to halt. Despite his best efforts, the car shivered to a stop some six feet from where she was standing.

No sooner did the woman climb aboard than she lit into Bill at the top of her voice. "Such inconsideration! Such atrocious service! Such downright incompetence on the part of the motormen!" Catching her breath, she began again, "Your streetcars are a disgrace! When are you going to quit running these cattle cars, anyway?"

Bill, who had been listening with apparent unconcern, smiled pleasantly and replied, "I reckon when the cattle quit riding them, ma'am."

—Helen Ogden Lawrence

Jest Plain Folks

John Doe

A sudden snowstorm left members of the Venison Club weather-bound in their hunting lodge, and, as they soon found to their misery, at the mercy of a new member who fancied himself as a yarn spinner. By mid-afternoon the others could recite every tedious detail of everything he had ever done on every one of his deer hunts.

The snow continued steadily, and so did the great hunter's accounts of his exploits. By nightfall the bore shifted to descriptions of his many deer rifles. After dinner he launched into detailed discussion of his hunting wardrobe.

"My greatest problem," he droned on, "is finding the right kind of cap. I've tried all kinds, but can't decide which is best. If the snow lets up tomorrow, what do you fellows suggest I wear?"

In a weary voice came one word, "Antlers."

—J. Bryan III

. . .And Justice For All

The customer began by being sharp and suspicious, and soon became quarrelsome. The hulking, amiable salesman was polite as could be, but it was no use. The customer's voice rose so high that the new floor manager strode over. Obviously bent on impressing the rest of the staff, he bawled out the salesman. Then, without giving the man a chance to say a word, he fired him on the spot. "No one," he announced, "should ever forget that the customer is always right."

Several months later the floor manager walked out of the store and right into a policeman who was tagging his car for overtime parking.

While the policeman was still bent over, fastening on the tag, the floor manager began giving him a terrific argument. When the policeman straightened up, the manager recognized him as the salesman he had fired.

"Oh," he said limply, "I didn't know you found another job."

"Yes," said the policeman. "And on this job the customer is always wrong."

—Henry Charles Suter

Bare Subsistence

The couple first met at a public swimming pool, where his fancy diving made him a hero. The following summer they were married, and soon began raising a junior swimming team.

Meanwhile, it dawned on the wife that her husband was close-fisted with his cash—so much so that she was still wearing trousseau dresses after nearly six years of marriage. Neither gentle hints nor sharp jabs, however, got across the idea of a clothing allowance. Her he-man husband remained completely blind to the fact that a woman occasionally needs new clothes, and that hers were both worn and dated.

She was almost in tatters one warm day when he asked, "Why don't you take the children down to the pool?"

"I'd like to," she said, "but I need a new bathing suit."

"Why?" he demanded. "What's wrong with the old one?"

"Oh, not much," she said, "except for a big hole in the knee."

—Mrs. Ethel Jenkins

Jest Plain Folks

Ups and Downs

The elevator was stuffy and overcrowded. Worse still, the operator persisted in plunging his vertical bus at full speed and jerking to an abrupt halt at the desired floor. Several passengers, visibly jarred, told him off pointedly as they got out. This only made it worse for the others. As he slammed the elevator to a standstill at the next floor, he glared at the shaken riders and said sarcastically, "*Hope* I didn't stop too suddenly."

An equally caustic voice from the rear of the car replied, "Why, of course not. I always wear them around my ankles."

—*E.C. Cearley, Jr.*

If the Shoe Fits

Mrs. Gottwealth, having suddenly inherited a small fortune, considered herself too good for the small town in which she lived. Her attitude created havoc in the town's one modest department store. She swept through it several times a week, seldom purchasing much, but always leaving merchandise in chaotic piles and clerks unnerved.

One hectic day, in the shoe department, she glared in disgust at the litter of shoes she had tried and discarded. "Why I bother to come here, I don't know," she proclaimed. "This store never has a thing that I can use—absolutely nothing."

The weary clerk looked up and managed a little smile. "No doubt you're right," he said politely, "but have you noticed our nice manners?"

—*Kerry Caine*

Brotherly Love

The latest addition to the neighborhood circle was an attractive young single woman who was well aware of her charms. She managed to keep so many married men in a tizzy that the neighborhood wives soon banded together to get her safely paired off. The young woman, however, neatly snubbed every eligible man to whom she was introduced. Without appearing too deliberate, she let it be known that she did not think much of their appearance, intelligence or social grace, as the case might be.

She was playing her role of the snobbishly discriminating female when she was introduced one evening to a thoroughly likable, quiet young bachelor. After alternately ignoring and chiding him all evening, she overheard someone mention that he had a very attractive brother. So, as he was about to leave, she said pointedly, "By the way, I hear you have a very handsome brother. I do hope you'll bring him around."

"Gladly," the young man said, "if you have a pretty sister."

—Mary P. Howley

Something Old, Something New

Young Mrs. Rallon came into the community club like an impatient tornado, vocally windy and destructive to any obstacle in her path. She was very critical of all old customs and plans.

"What we need," she announced firmly, "is young ideas. We're in a rut; we're worshiping the old, ignoring the new. For

Jest Plain Folks

example, one thing we simply must have is a youth center, a place where our children can go." Having established this fact, Mrs. Rallon proceeded to give detailed instructions for its operation, silencing all objections with a casual wave of her hand.

"We must have a young person to run this youth center," she said finally, "someone young enough to know what teenagers really like to do."

"And old enough," one of the older women said dryly, "to see that they don't do it."

—*Mrs. A.W. Johns*

Kid Stuff

Mr. Bigg, president of the Parent-Teacher Association, sought to rally support for a school bond issue. At the P.T.A. meeting he outlined an approach to be used in soliciting votes by telephone. Then, as if his audience were dim-witted, he ordered amiable Bob Smiley to "write it up on the blackboard for all to see." Smiley, whom Bigg took pleasure in embarrassing, obligingly chalked up the following gems as Bigg dictated them:

1. "My name is ——."
2. "I am calling in behalf of the P.T.A. about the bond issue."
3. "Are you registered to vote?"

At that point, Bigg obviously forgot his lines and paused. Smiley, who had suffered quietly through Bigg's condescending performance, delighted the meeting by suggesting the next line:

"May I please speak to your daddy?"

—*Minnie Hitov*

No-Line Nylons

During the wartime shortage of nylon stockings a certain United States senator was sent by his wife to a department store which had mailed its good customers "nylon tickets" entitling each to buy two pairs of the scarce hose.

When the senator arrived he found the stocking counters mobbed by frenzied women waving coupons. Although known as a fearless fighter on the floor of Congress, he decided to wait until the female battling subsided.

Nearly an hour later he realized that it was not going to let up. So he plunged into the horde of women, pushing and shoving and ignoring complaints. Finally he wedged himself in between two indignant matrons in front of the counter.

"Of all the nerve," one said. "You almost knocked me over. Can't you wait your turn? Why don't you act like a gentleman?"

As angry female voices rose in agreement, the senator said in his best speech-making voice, "Madam, I've been acting like a gentleman for nearly an hour and it got me nowhere. That's why I'm now acting like a lady."

—Erica M. Cromley

Jest Plain Folks

Heaven Can Wait

One of the student speakers at the college forum was a sincere young man bent upon proving the certainty of life after death, complete with bodily resurrection. While most of his undergraduate audience listened in silence, one young man, known for his irreverence and wild behavior, suddenly interrupted.

"How am I going to put on my shirt over my wings?" he demanded, and roared at his own joke.

Encouraged by a few snickers, he kept repeating his question until everyone was disgusted. Refusing to stop even then, he called out again, "Will I be able to get a shirt on over my wings?"

"Don't worry about that," a girl in the audience finally retorted. "Your problem is how to put your pants on over your tail."

—*Bill Fogarty*

Ruffled Feathers

Next to chattering in a featherheaded way, Mrs. Tom's chief hobby was criticizing clergymen. They were either too young or too old, too quiet or too talkative. If they were none of these, she managed to invent a few things to be critical about.

Once after listening to a fine sermon by the church's newest pastor, she cornered a fellow worshiper and gave her a lengthy explanation of just what was wrong with the minister. "You know," she said finally, "I just don't get anything from his sermons that I can carry home with me."

"Perhaps, Mrs. Tom," her weary listener said, "you don't bring anything to put it in."

—*Ruth Lewis Richardson*

Time Out

Mrs. Lawdeedaw, wife of a man who made himself a millionaire during World War II, never quite got accustomed to the luxury of having a large staff of servants. She took every opportunity to show off her butler along with her antiques. She had a profusion of white-capped maids serving on even the smallest social occasions, and made it plain to her guests that they were not simply hired for the afternoon. When her other conversation ran out, as it often did, she chattered at length about the servant problems involved in maintaining a large staff.

At an afternoon tea which she consented to hold for a none too wealthy or social group of charity workers, Mrs. Lawdeedaw suddenly realized that she might be overstressing the subject of numerous servants to virtual strangers who had few if any.

"Well, you know, we are very democratic about it all," she proclaimed. "We let *all* our servants go for two days a week."

"That's nothing," replied a modestly dressed young woman who had only a two-days-a-week cleaning woman. "We let ours go *five* days a week."

—Olney Rhode

Jest Plain Folks

Pest-aside

Everyone at the garden party was having a wonderful time except the guest of honor, a pretty out-of-town girl in her twenties. From the moment she arrived, she was pursued by the town's perennial bachelor, a seedy character nearly three times her age. He introduced her as "the girl I've been waiting for," interrupted her conversations with others, kept the younger stags at bay and almost drowned her in punch.

As the party drew near a close, it looked as if the persistent bachelor was winning despite all her efforts to escape. He had her sitting on a garden bench with not another man within 20 feet. Leaning close to her to press his advantage, he murmured:

"The perfume you have on has a haunting fragrance. I think I recognize it."

"You should," she said coldly. "It's insect repellent."

—Ann McFate

Chignon Chagrin

Gertrude was as contrary as a mule, though more attractive. When short hair was the fashion, she wore her long tresses piled high in a bun on the back of her head. If no one noticed it, she introduced the subject of hair into every conversation in hopes of drawing compliments.

Stopping in a millinery shop just before closing time, she helped make life miserable for the salesgirl who was already struggling to please two other customers. As she tried on one hat after another, she complained prettily about the agonies of finding one to go with "all this hair." Finally she put on a pixy-ish model with a pointed crown which covered the troublesome bun becomingly.

"It's so hard to decide," she pouted, "when this hides my very best feature. Honestly now, do you think this hat really does anything for me?"

"Certainly, madam," the salesgirl replied. "It makes your head look normal."

—Mary P. Howley

13

Skirting the Issue

As summer came to a chill end, the regulars in the rocking-chair brigade at the resort hotel closed ranks and finally consisted of single ladies who seemed to be discovering, unhappily, that life doesn't always begin at 40 or thereabouts. The more they rocked, the more they rapped. A favorite target for their caustic comments was the prettiest girl in the neighborhood. They criticized the way she dressed, the way she laughed, and the way all the men, attached and unattached, played up to her. Nor did they make any secret of their disapproval.

One evening as the girl came past their rocking chairs, a wind caught her ballerina skirt and twirled it in a revealing circle.

"When I was that age," one of the critics spoke out righteously and audibly, "young ladies never dreamed of going around with their skirts around their necks."

"I imagine," the girl replied cheerfully, "that the hoops helped to hold them down."

—*Richard Attridge*

Queen (11) B

The shapely young lady in Apartment 11-B treated the building employees as if she were the dowager queen of a despotism. She was especially rude and demanding with the quiet, yet harmless, old night doorman.

One Sunday while the maintenance man was out eating, a

Jest Plain Folks

break in the basement water connections left the apartment house dry. The doorman was repairing it, unaided, when his telephone jangled. It was the queen in 11-B. Without permitting the doorman to get in a word of explanation, she went into a tirade. Finally she shouted, "Do something, you old blockhead! I was in the shower covered with soap when the water went off."

"If you'll get off the phone and go back to your shower," he said politely, "in about five minutes I'll rinse you off."

—*Zebley Dawson*

Wrong Turn

Charles was an excellent driver whose years of experience gave him a casual sureness at the wheel. His friends recognized this, but not so his bride, Martha. Although she did not know how to drive, she ceaselessly directed and warned him. This kept up, much to his embarrassment, regardless of who was in the car with them.

When Charles, in self-defense, decided to teach his wife to drive, her know-it-all attitude made this difficult. One evening on the way to a party with another couple, however, she suddenly insisted on taking the wheel. "Never mind my gown," she announced. "You go sit on the back seat with Alice."

At a busy intersection, Martha stalled the engine and piled up traffic. Helplessly she wailed, "What must I do now?"

"I'm sure you'll remember," Charles said evenly, "if you'll just move back here."

—*Ken Ezinga*

Pampered Papooses

The desk clerk was rushed, and the woman, who had just come into the hotel with two young boys, was obviously impatient. While she indicated her impatience by drumming her fingers on the counter, her sons romped noisily around the lobby, jumping onto chairs, pulling open drawers and sliding back and forth on the polished floors.

"Be careful of your clothes," she called when one of her sons lifted an inkwell and spilled some of its contents on a rug. Then, turning to the harried clerk, she announced loudly, "I can't keep my boys waiting any longer! I have a reservation!"

"Yes, madam," the clerk said, then paused as one of the boys sent a smoking stand clattering to the floor. "And will you need help getting those two savages back on it?"

—*Kenneth F. Neilsen, Sr.*

Bearded Wonder

Even on a clear day Wilbur was an unnerving sight. But viewed in the rain, his wispy beatnik beard, stained trousers and sloppy jersey made him something to try to forget. So, when he

Jest Plain Folks

approached the attractive young lady standing under an awning at the summer resort, she understandably edged away.

Undisturbed, Wilbur promptly started telling her all about himself. He explained how disgusted he was with his conservative parents, the summer resort and the world in general. He went on to grumble about the weather. "Just what can a fellow like me do," he said, frowning at the rain, "on a day like this?"

The young lady gave him one more careful look, then said, "Mildew."

—G. *Ellsworth Harris*

Lost and Found

A rather scatterbrained young lady recently visited the home of her fiance's wealthy spinster aunt for the weekend. While unpacking her bag, she discovered to her dismay that she had brought a worn and badly faded pair of pajamas. Eager to make a perfect impression, and a bit awed by the elderly Victorian-looking maid who attended her, the young lady hid the pajamas under her mattress after she arose on the first morning.

Waking late the second morning of her visit, she dressed hurriedly and completely forgot about hiding the pajamas until after breakfast.

Then, giving her fiance and her hostess a hasty excuse, she rushed upstairs, only to find her bed already made and the stern-looking maid dusting the room. She stooped quickly and peered under the mattress.

"If you're looking for the pajamas, miss, you needn't worry," the maid said calmly. "I put them back in the young gentleman's room."

—*Frances Rodman*

Snide Swipe

Old Mr. Wilde, whose memory was as short as his temper, got into his car after an evening meeting and started homeward. As he came to the first intersection, a car from the side street missed him by inches.

Roaring like a cracked boiler, Wilde jumped from his car and started giving the other driver a large piece of his mind. Having called him a public menace and a threat to life, Wilde expanded on his carelessness and stupidity.

When Wilde finally paused for breath, the other driver spoke for the first time. "Are you finished?" he asked.

"Well, yes," Wilde sputtered.

"Then," the other said quietly, "I'd like to suggest that when you drive at night you turn on your lights."

—*Elizabeth Norris Hauer*

Fair Game

For years, it has been traditional for Uncle Rob to invite his contemporaries, fine, elderly sportsmen, to hunt pheasants with him on the opening day of the season on our family's small, well-stocked preserve near San Francisco. They hunt in a line, walking across the flat countryside, flushing birds, and the hunter nearest the pheasant gets the shot.

Somehow, a very brash and cocksure young man attached himself to one of these parties. Before the start, the young outsider regaled everyone with tales of his fishing and hunting prowess. Fifteen minutes later, it became painfully obvious that he never had hunted pheasants before. He blazed away regardless of whether it was another man's shot, whether the bird was in range or whether it was a cock or hen. Between times he popped away at hares, hawks and even stray blackbirds. If it flew or moved, he shot.

These one-man fusillades scared away the pheasants and ruined the hunting, but the disgusted sportsmen in the party were too polite to tell off the trigger-happy pest. Late in the day, however, one tired old gentleman climbed down into a drainage ditch and up the other side, instead of jumping across with the rest of the party. Instantly the pest twitted him on getting old.

"Young man," he replied bitterly, "I am not so much old as afraid—if I get both feet off the ground you might shoot me."

—*Ethel Rawlings Malcolm*

Pow (Wow!)

When the cross-country bus halted at a New Mexico restaurant, the passengers were pleasantly surprised to be greeted by a shapely hostess of obvious Indian extraction. One noisy young man, however, was too much carried away. Throughout lunch he voiced such witticisms as, "Me great white scout, you pretty Indian maiden, someday we make whoopee?"

The young lady bore this ordeal with the stoic calm of a true Indian. In a last effort to break her silence, the noisy one said, "Come on, Pocahontas, favor me with a phrase or two of your quaint native dialect."

At that, the girl looked straight at him and said, "Ugh!"

—*Charles A. Peters*

Objection Overruled

The hard-hitting out-of-town lawyer who was trying an accident case in our town felt sure he would win—until the beloved old town doctor testified for the other side. Realizing that he had to discredit the general practitioner's testimony somehow, the lawyer waged a clever campaign to make it appear that the elderly doctor was out of touch with modern medicine and woefully ignorant of scientific advances.

"Now tell me, doctor," he began each question gently. With each, he placed the old man in an increasingly awkward position. Finally he posed what he expected to be a crusher.

"Nowadays there is scarcely any such thing as a general practitioner," he said. "Medicine is highly specialized. Tell me, doctor, in what field do you specialize?"

With a faint smile, the general practitioner replied, "In the skin and its contents, sir."

—David St. John

Diving Bored

As a freshman in college, Joe Prator felt immeasurably superior to everyone in his own high school. So when he took a girl to the high school swimming meet, he spent most of his time telling her how much faster he could swim than any of the high school contestants.

Jest Plain Folks

Later, when the diving events were being run off, Joe grew even more expansive. Interpreting his companion's silence as awed admiration, he gave her a lengthy description of all his diving feats at college. "Why, last week," he said, "I did a double somersault from the high board and ended by diving through an inner tube floating on the water."

Turning to stare at Joe, the girl said wonderingly, "And your head squeezed through?"

—*Theodore G. Messner*

A Shady Deal

It sometimes gets unbearably hot during the University of Wisconsin summer school sessions at Madison, as I can testify from having been a student there. One stifling night everyone in a certain campus rooming house for men wore an irreducible minimum of clothing while studying. For added relief, the window shades were up.

There came a knock at the door, and someone handed in a note. It was from the girls in the dormitory across the way. Temperatures shot up on reading it.

"Dear boys," it said, "your course in anatomy is not appreciated. What's the matter with your window shades?"

The rooming house boys promptly composed a reply:

"Dear girls: The anatomy course is optional. Your windows have shades, too."

—*Irving S. Quale*

Henpecked

In all the years that Pete had been selling groceries to Mrs. MacGrump, he never completed a sale without having to answer at least one fussy question. Selling her a dozen eggs was always a trying experience, for Mrs. MacGrump would insist on holding each one up to the light and turning it over and over. Then she would demand, "Are you *sure* they are fresh?"

Pete put up with this performance patiently because Mrs. MacGrump usually shopped when there were few or no other customers present and he could devote himself to stilling her suspicions. One day, however, she arrived when the store was crowded, and delayed all the other customers. Pete tried in vain to hurry her along.

"Are you *sure* these eggs are fresh?" she finally challenged.

"Sh-h-h," he whispered, loud enough for the other customers to hear, "the hen doesn't know that I have them."

—*Cyrus B. Dingman*

Take Stock, Madam

After addressing a meeting of stockholders, an eminent corporation executive was questioned by some obviously sincere individuals and also by some who simply wanted to crowd into the

Jest Plain Folks

limelight. One pompous, overdressed woman, determined to impress everyone with her wealth and position, monopolized the discussion and finally said, "I don't quite know what to do with my block of stock. Conditions are so unsettled that the old rules just don't apply any longer. Now, as an official of the corporation, what is your advice?"

The executive, after pausing as though he was giving the matter considerable thought, replied, "Madam, if I were you, I would sell one share and keep the other."

—Bob Myers

Hold the Rains

Back when carriages were common in Vermont, a well-dressed woman in a smart-looking buggy was caught in a sudden thundershower. To escape the gusty rain, she guided her horse toward a tool shed beside the road.

As she approached this shelter, a farmer stepped out and held up his hand. "You can't drive under this shed, lady!" he called.

"I'd like to know why not!" the lady snapped. "You don't suppose I'm going to stay out here and be soaked!"

When the man continued to shake his head, she swelled with visible irritation. "Apparently you don't know who I am," she said crisply. "I'm Mrs. Railtod, of Morton!"

"I don't doubt it, lady," the farmer said, shifting his mild gaze to the top of her buggy. "But that don't make the shed no higher."

—Patricia Chase

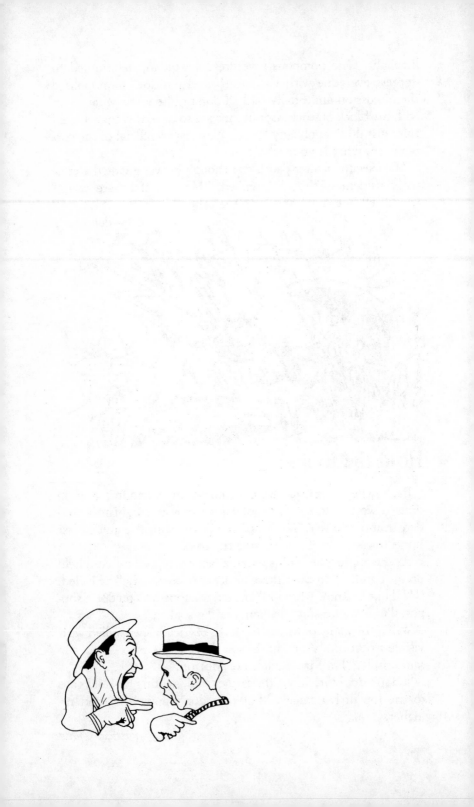

No Place Like Home

Wild, Wild West

Marilyn, who never had visited in the West, was more than outmatched in this respect by her mother, who had never even let her thoughts wander west of the Hudson. So when a college friend from the Rocky Mountains area invited Marilyn out for the holidays, her mother developed no small amount of reservation. She worried over travel conditions, blizzards and avalanches and acted in general as if her darling daughter were about to brave an untamed frontier.

The college friend and her parents, in long-distance calls, tried to calm the mother's fears. With every cause for concern eliminated, however, the mother still balked.

Finally the chum's mother said, "If it is hostile Indians you're worried about, let me reassure you—we live inside the fort."

—*Ann Brown*

Jet Set

The young Oklahoman, vacationing in New York City, was invited to a party of the sophisticated set and soon found himself cast in the role of country cousin or rustic clown. One sardonic man about town, in particular, questioned him at length for the amusement of the big-city dwellers.

"And do you drive your own car?" the wit asked. . . . "You do! Why, I'm amazed. I thought all you oil-wealthy Oklahomans had your own private chauffeurs."

"Oh, no," the youngster replied easily. "Only a few have chauffeurs—the rest have pilots."

—Charles Fenton

Space Race

Well irrigated with vodka, the Russian was boasting about Soviet supremacy in scientific fields. He had told his small, bored American audience about the first Sputnik, described in detail how the Russians trained a dog for the second satellite. Next he began a long, rambling lecture on Russia's plans for

No Place Like Home

putting men on future spaceships and satellites.

"Our men are eager for this adventure," he said finally. "They do not hang back. They really want to travel to outer space. Why, right now we have thousands of volunteers anxious to man future spaceships—far more than America has."

As he paused, a single weary voice was heard. "You could be right," one of his listeners said. "Very few Americans are that desperate to get out of the country."

—*D. O. Flynn*

Altar-nate Lifestyle

Kay Kato.

The campus belle, ever eager to outdo her rivals, soon paraded before them with the handsome exchange student from Iran. She helped him with his English, lunched with him and showed off her prize at every opportunity. To jolt her, one of the other coeds informed her that under Iranian law a man might have as many as six wives.

That evening at a social gathering, the belle confronted her Iranian and asked whether it was true. "Not any longer," he said thoughtfully, "but the practice did have its advantages." A snicker at the belle's expense ran around the gathering.

"Well," she stormed, "I suppose you feel you might grow tired of just one woman. Isn't that awfully egotistical? A woman might grow tired of you, too."

"That," the Iranian replied, "is what the other five are for."

—*Maxine L. Henry*

27

Con-fusion

The New England lady was traveling by train through the deep South during the early 1930s, when jails were often well-peopled with transients picked up on vagrancy charges. She soon made it plain that she did not like what she saw of the countryside. Beckoning to the conductor, she began delivering a lecture to that patient man.

"I must say that the North is far ahead of the South in many respects," she declared. Waving toward the passing landscape, she added, "Just look at those broken-down fences. And those shabby, paintless houses, so sadly in need of repair. Your Southern farmers must be a shiftless sort."

To all of which the conductor made no reply, but continued on through the car as soon as he could.

As he passed the lady's seat on the way back she stretched out a detaining hand.

"Look!" she cried, pointing triumphantly through the train window. "See that well-kept fence and those neat white farm buildings? See how unlike the South? Northern effort and energy must be responsible for that!"

The conductor smiled. "You're pretty nearly right, ma'am," he drawled. "Lots of Yankees do work there from time to time. That's our state prison farm."

—*Jewel Goodwin*

No Place Like Home

South of the Border

As the train rumbled across the prairies of Western Canada, the American visitor talked on and on. The Canadian who shared the table in the dining car listened politely, but he soon resented the stranger's air of superiority.

When the American made a particularly derogatory remark about the comparative dullness of Canadian political life, the Canadian spoke up.

"If you'll pardon my frankness," he said, "I think your political party conventions are a mild form of mass insanity."

"Ah, but that's where you're wrong!" boomed the American. "What you backward Canucks call insanity is really our genius for organizing and whipping up enthusiasm. And after all," he added knowingly, "there's only a thin dividing line between genius and madness."

"A very thin line," agreed the Canadian. "We in Canada call it the 49th Parallel."

—Lou McCartney

Birds of a Feather. . . .

Years ago there held forth in Southern Texas a real estate broker who extolled the beauties of the surrounding country-side so eloquently that he left even Californians and Floridians spellbound. Once he got started, there usually was no stopping him until he made a sale.

One day, however, he harangued a Northern visitor at great length without visible results. While they were on a sightseeing trip through an undeveloped section thick with underbrush, a long-tailed Texas bird known as a roadrunner scooted across in front of the car.

Showing a little interest for once, the Northerner asked, "What kind of a bird is that?"

The real estate man rose to the opportunity with a flourish. "That, suh," he said, "is a bird of paradise, no less."

"Well," the Northerner replied, "he's an awfully long way from home."

—James E. Tassell

Down on the Farm

Tom, an American university student, was admitted to the Soviet Union last summer with a small group of European tourists. As the only American in the group, he tried to be a model of quiet behavior. But their guide continually belittled "backward, capitalistic America" with some rather pointed asides in Tom's direction.

The guide's raptures reached a peak at the Agricultural Exhibit in Moscow. "In farming, as in all else," he proclaimed, "the Soviet Union cares for its people. Ultimately the Communist Party will provide ten times as much of everything for the people as does capitalistic America."

"That's already true in one respect," Tom spoke up. "In my whole state, there's only one prison farm."

—*George Carson*

Bum Steer

Two fancily dressed female tourists in a car with an Eastern tag somehow got off the highway far enough to become stuck in a mud hole. A cowboy rode up. Before he could offer help, the driver called, "What'll you charge to pull my car out?" Ignoring what he regarded as an insulting question, the rider dismounted, jacked up the rear of the car, scooped out mud, and jammed branches and rocks under the wheels. Meanwhile, he could hear the driver audibly worrying about how much she might have to pay him.

Tying his lariat to the front bumper, he remounted, advised the driver to gun the motor gently when she saw the rope tighten, and quickly rolled the car out of the hole. When he came back to untie his rope, the woman vaguely waved a five-dollar bill in his direction.

"It was a lot easier than I expected," she said. "I don't suppose you really earned this, but it's the smallest I have."

"Keep it, madam," the cowboy said dryly. "I would have done the same for a cow."

—S. Omar Barker

Peak Performance

Two Chinese Communist delegates to an international conference were angrily discussing the British Commonwealth feat of conquering Mount Everest. One of them denounced the accomplishment as an evidence of British imperialism. He asserted the British flag was planted on the peak not merely as a mountain-climbing gesture, but in a brazen infringement of native sovereignty.

Seeking to make as big an issue as possible, the Chinese turned to a British representative who happened to be nearby and said, "Isn't it one of your typical land grabs?"

"Really, I am not qualified to give an official opinion," the Britisher replied politely, "but I can say this: If you don't like the flag flying up there, why not climb up and take it down?"

—R. White

31

Pride and Prejudice

Air Cadet Rich was enjoying his first party in the South until one of the other guests, somewhat the worse for sociability, started riding him about his Northern background. After refighting the Civil War for a time, this noisy Southerner announced, "I'm from the biggest and best city in the South! Where you from boy?"

"A small town in Pennsylvania," Rich said.

"Some whistle-stop we never heard of down here, I guess."

"No," Rich said, "I think you've heard of it."

The Southerner snorted. "I doubt it, son, but tell us the name, anyway."

"Gettysburg."

—J.J. Taylor

Southern Hospitality

The young man with the Texas license plate on his coupe had made three trips around the Los Angeles block, looking for a parking place, when a car just ahead of him pulled out from the curb. As he slowed to pull into the vacant place, a horn tooted impatiently behind him. Turning, he saw a young woman in a long convertible waving violently for him to go on. "I want that parking place," she called. "Move on."

When the undaunted Texan continued to pull into the place, she blew her horn several times more. Then, pulling up beside his coupe, she glared at him and said, "I thought Texans were supposed to be polite."

"Thank you, ma'am," the Texan said, lifting his hat. "Any time you're in Houston you can be *my* guest."

—Lanna Folena

No Place Like Home

Southern Fried

Southern girls are constantly annoyed at Northerners who cling to the idea that we are all old-fashioned, beruffled damsels, straight out of a magnolia garden, who must be treated with extreme care and exaggerated gallantry.

Years ago, when I went up from Richmond to New York to be a bridesmaid in a schoolmate's wedding, I encountered this situation at its worst. The ushers were all Harvard men—not a bad thing in itself—but one of them insisted upon calling me "you-all," roaring with delight every time I opened my mouth. Soon he had me feeling like the comedy relief of the entire occasion.

"Sugar," he breathed down my neck at the wedding party, "you are for me. I'm going to take you like Grant took Richmond." Enchanted by this brilliant comparison, he boomed loudly, "Yes, sir, boys, I'm going to take this little girl just like we Yankees took Richmond. . . . How about it, honey?"

"Mercy," I cried, "do you mean that I have to put up with four years of this?"

—*Virginia W. Cann*

33

Measuring Up

The old Scots engineer was being conducted around an English marine-engineering plant by a brash, self-confident young Londoner, who never missed a chance of forcing home on the old man the great strides that the trade had made during the past 20 years or so.

"Of course," said the young man, "in your day, you didn't require a university degree to practice engineering, or a genuinely scientific training to work in a workshop. In fact, I'm told you didn't even know how to work to thousandths of an inch. Your generation never worked to such precisions as thousandths of an inch, did it?"

"No, *mon*," said the old Scot thoughtfully. "We just had to make it exactly right."

—*Renson Olwell*

Jolly Good Show

As the party progressed, its conversation was monopolized by one marathon talker. This man, an actor and television performer, used an extremely English accent with upper-clawss intonations. Although actually from the American Corn Belt, he

No Place Like Home

scoffed at most things American and obviously regarded himself as veddy superior, indeed.

At one point, he gleefully mimicked a girl from Kansas. Imitating her drawl and twang, he suggested that she enroll in "a good Eastern college, if there is one," and learn to speak English.

"Listening to me," he added unguardedly, "you'd never guess that I came from Kansas myself, now would you?"

"True," the girl replied. "And don't think Kansas doesn't appreciate it."

—*Raymond L. Marshall*

Snow Job

A real estate agent, seeking to sell land in Southern Texas to a group of frost-bitten Kansans, gave them an elaborate buildup about "The Land Where the Sunshine Spends the Winter," and then brought them down to see the region last January—just as it was shivering through the coldest weather and heaviest snowfall ever recorded there.

The Kansans, in an unthawing mood, declared that if they had wanted snow they could have stayed in Kansas.

The real estate agent, desperate, suggested that they call over a 14-year-old boy and ask him how often he had ever seen snow.

"This is the first snow I've ever seen," the young Texan declared. As the agent brightened, the boy added: "But I've seen it rain twice."

—*Mrs. A.A. Wiede*

Word War III

Male Drop

The young Air Force second lieutenant had just been assigned to command a B-29 bomber and to fly it on to an overseas base. His enthusiasm was soon dampened, however, when he was introduced to an arrogant first lieutenant who was to fly with him as a passenger. This officer was quick to take every advantage of his superior rank.

In outlining the duties of various crew members, the second lieutenant innocently requested his passenger to take his turn at guarding the plane, loaded with baggage and equipment, whenever they stopped en route to their destination.

"You may be the pilot of this plane, and in command," the first lieutenant snapped indignantly, "but I am still the ranking officer. The only order you can give me is to bail out."

With a dead-serious expression, the second lieutenant replied, "Sir, I would advise you to wear your parachute at all times when we are in the air."

—*Jim Boyd*

Unsunk Hero

During one of the grimmest periods of the war, the British submarine *Sturgeon* was being escorted by a destroyer through the enemy-infested waters of the English Channel. As the entire French coast was in Nazi hands, Nazi aircraft and E-boats were continually attacking shipping. When the submarine approached the most dangerous part of the Channel, its young captain felt that he owed it to the escorting destroyer to indicate whether or not he would dive in case of attack.

Without giving a second thought to the fact that it smacked of bravado, he sent a signal with a heroic ring to it: "In the event of enemy attack, I intend to remain on the surface."

Seconds later, his face reddened as the destroyer flashed back: "So do I."

—M.R.G. *Wingfield, Commander, RN*

Neck and Neck

One ingrained belief held by many regulars, Army and Navy, is that the higher a man's rank, the higher his intelligence necessarily must be. By this reasoning, generals and admirals have the highest I.Q.'s on earth and are not to be questioned by anybody concerning anything.

The admiral who headed a Navy bureau in Washington during World War II was a prime example of this. Although his bureau handled many highly technical matters, he acted as if he knew far more about their intricacies than the experts who had devoted their whole lives to the work. By refusing to accept recommendations or to approve plans without numerous rejections and trivial corrections, he kept his staff in constant bewilderment. The work of the bureau lagged sadly.

Just then many regular Navy officers were ordered to sea and their places were taken by reserves with less blind respect for rank. Too, the admiral was prodded from higher up to speed up the bureau's operations.

Summoning the entire staff, he gave a lengthy talk on the necessity for streamlining procedures and accelerating work. "Wherever bottlenecks exist," he concluded, "I demand that you get rid of them. Any comments?"

"Sir," said an irreverent reserve officer with a reputation as a toper, "having had considerable experience with bottles, it is my observation that the necks are always at the top."

—*Francis Charles*

Survival of the Fittest

After a typical day at the Air Force survival school, which tried men's souls and made their muscles cry out, the older officers flopped thankfully on their bunks. Starting with calesthenics, they had packed each hour with painful action, including the obstacle course run at dusk. Now they asked only to rest.

Two very young and very buoyant lieutenants had other ideas. They persisted in bouncing around the barracks, taunting the older men about their lack of stamina. They called them "grampa" or "dad," wondered with mock solicitude about their rheumatism and generally acted like a couple of kids who had the day off from school.

The older men took the ribbing with silent patience, ignoring the most juvenile of the lieutenants' jokes and smiling aside the others. But finally, after an especially noisy outburst, one older captain released a long sigh.

"Children," he said quietly, "can be so cruel."

—*1st Lt. Henry L. Zeybel, USAF*

cdbean

Junior Achievement

No matter how much rank an officer has, the Army goes on the theory that it is never too late for him to go to school. In keeping up with the latest intricacies of modern warfare, a class of majors, lieutenant colonels and colonels was assembled at the artillery school at Fort Sill for a refresher course.

On the first day, these officers' jaws fell in one collective motion when there walked in to instruct them a young second lieutenant. As the lieutenant was not wearing his service ribbons, his students had no way of knowing that he had fought through World War II as an artillery sergeant before being appointed to West Point and commissioned. All they could see was that he was a very junior officer, who, presumably, couldn't tell them anything.

There was an audible mutter of disparagement and resentment as the lieutenant requested the class to come to order.

Word War III

Several officers rather ostentatiously got up and went out, while others looked annoyed.

Undaunted, the lieutenant faced the class and announced, "Gentlemen, there are thousands of men in the Army who know more about this course than I do. But I don't see any of them here, so I'll begin."

—J. D. Sewell

Down to Earth

In attaining a high rank in the National Guard, the local banker acquired a reputation as a ruthless martinet. He had served on the Mexican border as a youngster, but much of his duty in both World Wars had been at desks. To make up for his lack of combat service and his limited firsthand knowledge of new weapons, he relied upon reading military manuals and putting up a brusque front.

One day on an inspection tour, accompanied by a young lieutenant, he climbed onto the turret of a spotlessly shiny tank. Turning on his escort, he demanded, in a tone which mingled horror and triumph, "Lieutenant, is that dirt I see down there?"

"I think so, sir," the lieutenant replied cheerfully. "The bottom tank hatch is open, and you're looking at the ground."

—Merlin Nelson

Lowering the Beam

One of the instructors at an officer candidate school was an Air Force flier who brashly disregarded orders against classroom recruiting for any specific branch of the armed forces. He took every opportunity to devote lengthy portions of his lectures to stressing why the Air Force was superior to all other branches.

Not content with this, he began proselytizing the students during their very brief rest and recreation periods. One warm afternoon he walked up to a group who were waiting their turn at a tennis court, singled out one hapless young man, and proceeded to give him a sales talk for the Air Force.

Finally he asked the young man point-blank, "When you graduate, what branch of the service do you intend to enter?"

There was hushed attention as the youth replied, "Until I heard all that you had to say about the Air Force, sir, I hadn't made up my mind. But now," he added as the flier began to beam, "I've definitely decided—on antiaircraft."

—*Ronald M. Obach*

Band-aid

After a hard tour of duty, my battalion of Australians was in rest billets near Boulogne during the summer of 1917. Unexpectedly, our "vacation" was interrupted by orders to provide an honor guard at the Hotel de Ville, where high Allied officials were holding a conference. I was told off as commander of the guard and immediately readied my men for duty.

From early morning until 1:30 p.m., we stood rigidly under arms. Then word came that we would be relieved at 2:00 p.m. by a detail from the world famous Grenadier Guards. Our band, headed by an unreconstructed Irishman named O'Leary, was to play for the changing of the guard.

Promptly a glittering captain of the Grenadiers showed up to make it painfully clear to us that he wanted no slipshod "colonial" soldiering to mar the perfection of the occasion. He added that if our band happened to have the music to "The British Grenadier," that good old tune would be most appropriate. O'Leary swallowed this without a word.

At five minutes to two, the Grenadiers approached, feet all

slapping the pavement in unison, arms swinging shoulder high, web equipment shining with "blanco." Their captain halted them some distance away and came over with last minute suggestions to "improve" our formations. Finally satisfied, he went back to his men.

"Guards . . . 'shun!" his order crackled. "Quick . . . march!"

O'Leary, his Irish mug grinning, swung his baton. And the band crashed into the strains of "The Parade of the Wooden Soldiers."

—*George Fielding Eliot*

. PAUL LOKER .

Taking the Wrap

Everything ran wild in the hospital while the young Air Force physician was Medical Officer of the Day. From the emergency ward to the maternity delivery room, there was scarcely a quiet moment all night. Next morning, the young physician was exhausted when he turned in his routine report to the colonel who commanded the hospital. To his surprise, the colonel, after glancing at it, called for an explanation.

"See here, lieutenant," he snapped, "can you give me any logical explanation of why Maternity should have required twice the average number of diapers from Supply last night?"

"Only, sir," the lieutenant replied, "that this current crop of babies lacks respect for Government property."

—*Capt. Allen R. Robertson*

Who's Who

Early in the war, our company was caught short of food, short of sleep and short of equipment. Worst of all, though, we found ourselves constantly harassed by perhaps the most short-tempered officer in the whole Army. He was given to bellowing at the enlisted men for little or no reason, and shutting them up gruffly if they tried to reply.

One night this officer was assigned to make the rounds as orderly officer. Walking up to one weary sentry, he flashed his light in the man's face. When the sentry made no move, the officer demanded, "Why don't you challenge me, sentry?"

"Because I recognize you, sir," the sentry said.

At that the officer got blazing mad. "How the devil could you recognize me," he roared, "on a night as black as this?"

"Because, sir," replied the sentry, "I heard the sergeant tell the corporal that the orderly officer had swiped the only good flashlight in camp."

—*PFC. Roger M. Wood*

Bull's-eye!

The late Dixie Tighe, war correspondent for the *New York Post*, had a vast respect for fighting men, but no reverence for the spit-and-polish side of Army life. Once, while walking along a street in postwar Tokyo, she passed a platoon of white-helmeted military police standing stiffly at attention before their barracks. A young, self-important second lieutenant was going down the line, carefully inspecting each man's carbine. He would snatch the piece, peer into the breech, look down the barrel, then thrust it back to its owner with a frown that suggested he still was suspicious.

While he was peering lengthily into one barrel, Dixie paused directly behind him. "Honey," she said in a sweet but carrying voice, "it's a gun."

—*Ralph Chapman*

Follow the Leader

Sergeant McBlaak loved to talk, so he was delighted with his assignment as instructor in an Army school. He not only enjoyed being able to talk without interruption but also worked up a series of nerve-shattering devices to keep his listeners alert. He would blow a whistle to startle a nodding group, fire a cap pistol to emphasize a point, or ring a concealed cowbell to mark a correct reply.

During one lecture on the function of rank, noting some nodding heads, he shrilled his whistle and clapped his hands: "Now listen carefully, men. You have all been captured and interned. All the men in your prison compound are privates except one. He is a Pfc. Now think hard. Who gives the orders?"

From the rear of the room a bored voice sounded: "The enemy, sergeant."

—*Pvt. R. B. Stannard*

45

Salutations

Although famed for their fighting qualities, the New Zealanders bore the reputation of being the most casual and unsoldierly soldiers in the world when off the parade ground. To the horror of officers of "well-bred" armies, they often regarded military formalities with unconcealed amusement.

A top-ranking British officer who rode through the New Zealanders' area in Italy in his flag-bedecked car complained bitterly to their commanding officer, Lt. Gen. Sir Bernard Freyberg, "Not once did your men salute properly! Many of them simply stood and stared."

Sir Bernard, no stickler for military form in the field, considered gravely for a moment and replied, "Why didn't you try waving to them? I do, and they always wave back."

—*John Spedding*

Pulling Rank

On her first visit to the officers' club, the bride of a young second lieutenant found herself at a table with a group of other service wives. One older woman, to whom all the others deferred, was monopolizing the conversation with a long, glowing account of her husband's achievements. She stressed his special abilities, his many successes in the service and his skill and smartness in dealing with just about everything that came up.

Finally she turned to the lieutenant's wife with a bright social

Word War III

smile. "My husband is a colonel," she said, then paused, an obvious question in her eyes. "And yours——"

The unintimidated bride smiled right back. "My husband is 20," she said pleasantly. "And yours——"

—*Catherine R. Guy*

Name That Tune

While serving as a Navy doctor in the Pacific, I was driving a jeep through a driving rain on the lonely mountain road from Pago Pago to Mapusaga when I saw two burly enlisted marines sloshing along with packs and rifles. I stopped and told them to hop in the back seat.

We rode along wordlessly for a while. Then through the din of the rain I heard the marines whistling, in unison and in perfect key, a selection from one of Verdi's operas. A Japanese air raid couldn't have surprised me more.

The incongruity of the situation impelled me to say over my shoulder, "Here I thought you marines were tough guys who did nothing but fight and cuss and talk about women. And now on this forsaken island I hear you whistling an aria from *Rigoletto*. It's remarkable!"

Without a suggestion of insolence in his tone, one of the marines replied, "The only remarkable thing about it, sir, is that an officer recognized the tune."

—*Leon Bromberg, M.D.*

On the Spot

When Horace became a Military Police lieutenant, he sud-denly bloomed like an official cactus. Half his waking hours he spent studying rules and regulations, the other half in scurrying around enforcing even the least important of them.

One evening, while poking the spotlight of his patrol car into unlikely places, he saw a G.I. and a girl in friendly embrace. Al-though the street was deserted and the couple obviously were disturbing no one, Horace felt sure they must be breaking some regulation. So driving closer and carefully silhouetting them with his spotlight, he barked, "Break it up there, soldier! We can't allow any display of affection in public."

As the two parted, the girl turned into the light. "If you turn that light off," she said calmly, "we won't be in public."

—*John A. Brooks*

Standing Room Only

The interurban bus was jammed. Among the passengers standing wearily in the aisle during the long, hot ride was a lanky private just back from Korea. When a number of people got off at Shreveport, Louisiana, the private sank gratefully into an empty seat. The seat next to it—last one left—was quickly taken by a freshly pressed second lieutenant who had just boarded the bus.

The lieutenant had hardly got settled when he was met by the reproachful gaze of an elderly lady struggling to stay on her feet in the swaying bus. Discomforted, he turned to the private, who was blissfully resting. "Soldier," the lieutenant snapped, "why

Word War III

don't you offer that lady your seat?"

"I was about to, sir," the weary private said. "Then I remembered that the same Act of Congress that made me a soldier made you 'an officer and a gentleman.' "

—*Nell C. Gillis*

Chase Scene

There was good cooperation among the services in one of the major island invasions of the Solomons campaign—until near the end. Then a detachment of Army military police arrived and some of them began trying to run things behind the lines as if no war were going on. One MP, in particular, went out of his way to play traffic cop on a newly built road which the Seabees had constructed right into an advance area where the Marine Corps was still fighting the Japanese.

One morning the Seabee commander was hurrying along the road in his jeep, feeling a justified pride in the fine construction job, when the air was shredded by the shrilling of a siren. He found himself overtaken by the busybody MP in a police jeep.

"Pull over," the MP ordered. Then he got out and began in an exasperated tone, "Don't you know you can't go over 15 miles an hour on this road?"

"The hell we can't, son," the graying Seabee commander replied in exasperation. "We went faster than that when we built it, trying to keep up with the marines."

—*Capt. Walter W. Koenig, USMCR*

Flashback

It was right after the war, when everybody's chief concern was to get home as fast as possible and tempers snapped short at delays. Our battered old transport was crawling between Marseille and Norfolk, returning our troops.

As we churned slowly through the Strait of Gibraltar, the British shipping-control station high on the Rock challenged us via blinker light as if the war were still going on. "What ship? What ship?" they demanded.

We replied with our wartime code designation, plus our international call signal, which should have been sufficient. But the British, apparently not wanting to bother to look in the code books, stubbornly persisted in challenging us. Finally came a mandatory message, "Reply at once!"

At that, our skipper's hard-tried patience frazzled into fury. Through our glasses, we could see an embarrassed scurrying on the famous Rock when, just as the control station began another string of signals, "What ship? What ship?" We flashed back for all the world to see:

"Queen Mary. What Rock? What Rock?"

—Paul McKinnis

Rough Riders

The military transport plane, temporarily assigned to a self-important civilian on government business, ran into a violent thunderstorm over Brazil. To the crew, such storms were old stuff. With the copilot at the controls, the plane's captain, an easygoing Texan, relaxed in his seat with his shoes off for comfort. Before long the "very important" passenger barged into the cockpit, outpouring a barrage of questions.

"Isn't this weather dangerous?" he demanded.

The captain wiggled his toes and shrugged.

"Shouldn't we be flying a lot higher for safety?" the passenger persisted. "Don't you realize we're going over some of the roughest country in the world? This part of Brazil is very rocky, full of swamps and snakes——"

Just then a terrific downdraft dropped the swaying plane toward the earth with elevator speed.

Word War III

Clutching for support, the passenger shouted, "I knew it! We're going to crash, captain! What'll I do? Shall I bail out? What are you going to do?"

"Well," the captain said mildly, "if it's as rough down there as you say, I'm going to put on my shoes."

—G.R. *Roberts*

Command of the Language

Eager to try out his budding knowledge of German, Corporal Perkins spoke to the man nearest him in Munich's Hofbrauhaus. He started to explain in halting German that he had been studying the language only since being assigned to Germany a few months before. But the German quickly interrupted him to point out, in very good English, that his accent was atrocious and his grammar worse.

When Perkins tried to apologize and explain that he just wanted a little practice, he was interrupted again. The German said flatly that Americans had no linguistic ability. He went on to explain at length how quickly he had picked up English, how easily he had mastered the accent and the grammar. "Germans," he said finally, "are far superior to Americans in this respect. How else can you explain my perfect command of your language and your stumbling efforts at German?"

"Well, I guess you've had a lot of practice," the corporal said, "since 1945."

—*Lauren K. Bowen*

Close Encounters

During the war, some American and British bomber pilots were swapping stories about their experiences. The British, who had been blasting German targets for a long time before the Americans arrived, described a few of the many missions they had flown. And then a young Yank began lauding the exploits of his countrymen.

Though he had been over Germany only twice, he implied that the fearless tactics of the American fliers would soon prove far more effective than the—well, the pardonably cautious methods of the war-weary Royal Air Force. "We are really plastering them," he declared. "Take our last mission. Why, we went down as low as 8,000 feet before we let go our bombs!"

A veteran RAF flier, listening politely, seemed properly impressed. "I say, old boy, that's dangerous," he remarked. "Better tell your pilots never to go below 8,000 feet."

"The flak, eh?" the Yank said. "You mean it gets pretty thick down there?"

"There's that, of course," the Briton replied. "But if you chaps go below 8,000, you're going to start colliding with the Royal Air Force planes."

—*Donald B. Fernie*

Word War III

Taken to the Cleaners

The reconnaissance patrol, consisting of two light M-24 tanks and a few cars, pressed forward until halted by intense fire from a freshly established Chinese strongpoint in Korea. Having located the enemy, the patrol turned back. It passed through the friendly roadblocks marking the front line in somewhat more battered condition than it had started out.

Halted beside the road, just out of enemy range, was a newly arrived marine medium-tank platoon of M-26s; each was about twice the size of the light tanks. A marine sergeant, looking down on the little column from his M-26 turret, called out sarcastically to the reconnaissance patrol, "Hey, where did you get those peewee tanks?"

From one of the little tanks, the reconnaissance leader answered wearily, "Yours will shrink, too, sergeant, when they go through that Chinese laundry up there."

—*Capt. Kibbey M. Horne*

Wring Around the Collar

My rifle company had just come to a rear area after three months on the Korean front, when our platoon leader was replaced by a young second lieutenant fresh from Officer Candidate School. An extremely eager beaver, this lieutenant started right out by giving us long, boring lectures on everything he had learned in school.

Once, while droning on and on about first aid, he noticed that the medic assigned to our platoon, who happened to be a veteran of many battles, wasn't paying strict enough attention. So he made him get up and stand at attention. Later during this long lecture, thinking the medic's attention again was wandering, the lieutenant turned suddenly to him and said, "Suppose I had a severe head wound and was bleeding profusely. What would you do?"

Cheerfully, and very sincerely, the medic answered, "Sir, I'd put a tourniquet around your neck."

—*PFC. Robert H. Perkins*

Bars and Stripes

Our sergeant at Fort Ord, California, in 1944 was one of the few regular Army noncoms with combat service who failed to win a commission before returning home. Thoroughly soured, he took it out on us average soldiers and "4-F's in uniform," as we called ourselves. It soon became apparent that the sergeant was grimly determined to show up every other outfit as unsoldierly—and that we were going to be the guinea pigs for his demonstration of iron discipline.

One day the sergeant was holding forth on our unmilitary conduct, when some German prisoners of war came to work around the building. Spotting them, the sarge promptly quoted regulations forbidding conversation with prisoners of war. "In other words," he wound up sternly, "have nuttin' to do wit' dem guys. Get it?"

"Yeah," piped up a bespectacled little private. "But how do you tell them from the rest of us inmates?"

—*N.D. Christensen*

Eye Opener

The Navy eye specialist was capable, but not so good as he thought he was. To hear him talk, however, was to get the impression that he was the foremost eye doctor in the world.

"You're really lucky, boy," he told one youngster who was recuperating from a retina operation. "Why, in civilian practice

Word War III

I would. have charged you at least $2,000 for that operation. When you joined the Navy, you didn't make a mistake."

"No, sir, I didn't," the young man replied. "But it sounds like you did."

—Joyce Hawley Crews

Paying Attention

In taking care of its own, the Navy extends medical care and hospitalization to the dependents of naval personnel wherever possible. Since much of the Navy is based on the West Coast, the dependents' department of a large naval hospital there became badly overcrowded.

When a retired rear admiral whose wife was suffering from a relatively minor complaint insisted that she be hospitalized, the outranked medical officer in command of the hospital was reluctant, but finally gave in. He apologized for the overcrowding and said, "Admiral, we'll do the best we can, as usual."

The following day the admiral called and was indignant upon finding his wife in a double room with the wife of an officer far junior in rank.

Confronting the medical officer, he thundered, "Why is my wife put in a double room? Don't you people pay any attention to rank here?"

"Certainly, sir," the doctor replied, "What rank is your wife?"

—Jessie K. Gordon

CAVALLI

Supply and Demand

Having pushed her aggressive way to the checkout counter of the supermarket, Mrs. Stanhood herded her young son before her into the narrow slot and blocked his exit with her grocery cart. This limited his movements, but didn't stop them. Imitating his mother's tactics, he jostled the elderly woman ahead of him, stumbled on and off her toes a few times, and squirmed between her and the checkout counter.

Mrs. Stanhood ignored the elderly woman's discomfort. But when her son happened to jar her own grocery cart, she became suddenly critical.

"If you don't keep still, I'll put you on the counter and have the man sell you!" she snapped.

After she had repeated this loud threat a number of times with no effect, the elderly woman turned.

"Madam," she said quietly to Mrs. Stanhood, "there is no demand for your product."

—B. Declercq

All Kidding Aside

All Kidding Aside

Out on a Limb

One summer day, a retired British admiral, decorated for service in both World Wars and accustomed to commanding men, looked from a window of his country place and saw his two sons, aged nine and seven, in the branches of an apple tree happily munching green apples in direct disobedience to orders.

Flinging open the window, he shouted to the older boy, "Alfred, how many of those apples have you eaten?"

There was an uncomfortable silence that smacked of mutiny to the admiral.

He bellowed, "Alfred, don't you hear me? I am speaking to you! How many of those apples have you eaten?"

Whereupon the younger son, Gillis, slowly turned on the limb until he faced his father, and said with all the dignity of his seven years, "Please don't roar at him, Father—he's counting."

—*Charles R. Lesueur*

Editor's Note

When the headmaster's report came in, it showed the boy standing 49th in a class of 89—not disgraceful, but not good enough to suit his mother. She suspected that her son, who was attending a well-known Southern military academy, was not studying overly hard. She was about to write and tell him so, when she came across an editorial in the school paper. It called upon the cadets to realize that sending a boy to military school costs a lot of money, and means sacrifices for the parents. To fritter your time away, to read comic books during study periods, to make poor grades when you are capable of better ones—that, the editorial said, is cheating. Cheating your parents, cheating yourself. The cadet's mother discarded her plan of writing a scolding letter. Instead, she sent her son the editorial. "Read this carefully," she urged her boy. "Keep it in front of you. This boy is thinking."

She drew a prompt reply. "I wouldn't want it to get around," her son confided, "but I wrote the editorial."

—*Doris W. Daniels*

A Touch of Class

It was the pre-dinner period and Mrs. Staley, a woman who delighted in talking, was well launched on her favorite subject. "I simply adore formality in dining," she told her guests. "A well-appointed table means more to me than food. . . .Little touches like candles and flowers and the proper crystal and silver. These aren't trimmings to me; they're a necessary part of gracious living, really a part of our family pattern."

After continuing her unrequested lecture for far too long, Mrs. Staley rose to lead her guests to dinner. "I feel that dining formality is especially valuable for children," she said, pausing to pat the head of her small son, Billy. "It teaches them a natural love of the gracious and, of course, it gives them a true reflection of the family in which they live."

In the brief pause that followed, Billy's whispered comment to his father was all too clear. "Gee, dad, look," he said wonderingly; "we're eating in the dining room."

—B. J. Alford

59

Drummer's Snare

The community band conductor, a peevish type, took out most of his wrath on the band's quiet young snare drummer. He gibed at the boy continually for being a poor musician. One hot day at a public rehearsal, with many summer residents in earshot, the conductor overdid to the point of snapping his baton. As usual, he blamed the snare drummer.

"There, I broke it trying to teach you to play," he complained. "If a person is too stupid to play any other instrument, we give him two sticks and make him a drummer."

"Yes," the lad shot back, "and if he is so clumsy that he breaks one stick, he becomes a conductor."

—*Don Seibert*

Half and Half

In a small California town where everyone knows everyone else, a very pretty little girl walked out of a self-service store struggling with a large bag of groceries. Outside the store, regaling a group of loitering young men with his stories, stood the teenage town wit, a character with the latest fancy haircut and fancy pants.

"As pretty as you are," he teased the little girl, "some sharp guy would carry that bag home for you if you were 20."

"I'm ten," she said, "and a polite one might carry it halfway."

—*Glenell Thomas*

Trade Winds

The brightly decorated float, which held a very nervous small boy in a very large sailboat, was waiting to take its place in the parade when a group of horsemen paused beside it.

"Ahoy there, sailor," one of the parade riders called. "Watch out you don't tip that vessel over and drown."

The youngster managed a smile. The rider, enjoying his own humor, kept right on making comments. He wanted to know how many times the boy had been across the ocean, when he had started going to sea and where his oars were. Finally, raising his voice to increase his audience, the rider roared at the embarrassed boy, "Tell me, skipper, why don't you sail away?"

Just then the float began to move, and the youngster spoke for the first time.

"Not enough wind," he said clearly, "—until you came along."

—*Alfred M. Wolfe, Jr.*

Puppy Love

When ten-year-old Dian was given a puppy, her mother made it clear that she would have full responsibility for taking it outside whenever necessary. Dian agreed, and for some time carried out her assignment faithfully. Later, her enthusiasm waned. One night when she was wakened to do escort duty, she made tearful protests.

Her mother immediately reminded Dian of her promises. Then she went into a lengthy explanation of why people must keep promises, and how it builds character to do unpleasant things. Finally, as a clincher, she pointed out that she had had to do much the same type of thing for Dian when she was younger.

Fully awake by then, Dian moved to the door. "But you," she said coldly, "didn't have to take me outside."

—*Vincent Thomas, Jr.*

Relatively Speaking

Each time father took us children to the zoo, he would carefully explain that we must be on our best behavior. "Because," he would invariably add, "we are going to see your mother's relatives."

Mother, a wonderfully patient person, just smiled and endured it until the day when father elaborated on the joke.

"I wonder," he said that day, "if we will find your mother's grandfather chained in his cage."

Mother looked thoughtful. "It's really too bad that you

children won't be able to see your father's relatives."

"Why can't we see them?"

"Because, my dears," mother said quietly, "your father's relatives never could be captured."

—L. L. Stokes

And That's an Order

Young Mr. Bellott, who was an efficiency expert at heart, arranged the details of the family picnic as carefully as if he were taking a military unit into the field. Having double-checked the route, the food and the play equipment, and firmly vetoed most of his wife's and young son's suggestions as impractical, he herded them into the car.

At the picnic grove, while unpacking, he snapped a series of brisk orders to his son: "Put that down. . . .Leave that alone. . . .Get that blanket. . . .Don't touch that basket. . . .Stop poking in that bag. . . ."

His son obeyed the orders without comment. But, after a long period of silence, he asked in a small, bewildered voice, "Daddy, are we having a good time?"

—Mrs. Fred Lazzeroni

Rising Son

At first Jim's friends smiled at the way the gruff he-man suddenly became a doting father after the birth of his first boy. They listened to his stories patiently, time and again, with the indulgent air that kindly men usually wear toward new fathers.

But Jim, unfortunately, was so carried away by the novel experience of fatherhood that he kept buttonholing and annoying everyone. Finally he cornered a weary bachelor and babbled at length on the wonders of his son.

"And just imagine," he continued, "he's only 17 months old and he's been walking for nine whole months."

"Then," said the bored bachelor, "don't you think it's about time he sat down?"

—*Louise Forbes*

The Seven-Year Itch

Lawrence, aged seven, was summoned from a wonderful game with other boys to meet an old school chum of his mother's. The visitor immediately smothered him with kisses and hugs. Despite his gentle squirming, she held him in her clutch and asked question after question:

What class was he in? Did he like his teacher? Was he a good little boy in school? Did he play with little girls?

Finally the visitor demanded: "Tell me, Lawrence, what are you going to be when you grow up?"

"When I grow up," he said firmly, "I'm going to be let alone."

—*Harold Coffin*

Let Freedom Ring

The new second-grade teacher soon learned that what she took to be a moderately progressive school was an extreme institution for all-out freedom of expression by the pupils. The principal, an outspoken advocate of this system, constantly announced in the classrooms that teachers must never "repress" the little dears in any way. Thus encouraged, the youngsters made the place a bedlam.

For several weeks the new teacher watched helplessly while her little individualists expressed themselves by battering desks and furniture and smearing the freshly painted walls. Her suggestions that everyone should cooperate to keep the classroom attractive were regarded as a great joke.

When one obstreperous boy poured ink over her desk, however, it was too much. Grabbing him, the outraged teacher applied old-fashioned psychology to his seat of learning. Just then, the principal stalked in. Aghast, he demanded, "What goes on here?"

Without missing a lick, the teacher snapped back, "I'm just expressing myself."

—*D.B. Williams*

Beat the Clock

.CRAWFORD

By-line

Having just published her first book, an egotistic young woman writer set out to dazzle her less successful friends at the monthly gathering of their little group of struggling authors and poets. In contrast to their casual dress, she appeared in an expensive new outfit. Although the group had a reputation for forthright criticism and cutting remarks, she did her best to monopolize conversation. Whenever anyone told a story, she topped it. Whatever anyone else had done, she had done it too —and had written about it in her book.

With an intense expression on her hatchet-thin face, she asserted, "My experiences have covered such a wide field I have material for a number of books. Take aviation. Why, I was soloing at 14, doing stunt flying at 16, and by the time I was 20——"

A woman guest who could stand it no longer leaned forward intently. "Do tell them of your war record, darling," she said in a whisper that carried across the room. "Is it true that you were a test pilot for the American Broom Company?"

—*Champ Phillips*

RESSLER

Concrete Evidence

The head of the geology department at a Western engineering college was a brisk, businesslike scientist who felt he was there to teach, not to fraternize with the students.

Several pranksters in one of his classes were irritated by his aloof manner and his disdain of their wisecracks. They decided to show him up.

Obtaining a fragment of concrete from the materials-testing laboratory, they handed it to him just before his lecture one morning, said they had found it on a field trip and asked him to identify it.

The geologist looked at it carefully, bounced it on his palm several times and handed it back.

"I think," he said with a smile, "that it's a piece of damned insolence."

—*Arnold P. Wilking*

Beat the Clock

Teacher's Pest

Soon after the spring term began, the young teacher realized that the principal had unloaded the school's most unruly problem children on her. Being new, she hesitated to complain.

Then came the day when the principal smugly informed several important visitors to the school that she had some of the nicest pupils there—"all fine, normal youngsters."

"Is that so?" one of the visitors casually asked the teacher.

"Well, not quite," she replied with a smile. "Two are abnormal—they have good manners."

—Lloyd E. Graham

Wreckless Driving

The big man in the big new automobile fairly snapped with annoyance at the highway patrolman: "You stopped the wrong man this time. Save yourself the trouble of writing a ticket. I had lunch with the commissioner of highways. I golf with your patrol chief. The governor's secretary is my neighbor. So get on your bike and be on your way."

"Here is your ticket, sir," the patrolman replied. "You are charged with speeding, running a red light and reckless driving."

"Is that all?" the big man asked sarcastically.

"Yes, sir," the patrolman replied. "But only because there no such charge as 'driving under the influence of influence.'"

—Winston Johnson

69

Last Curtain Call

Young Mrs. Gavin's limited acting ability offered her a wonderful opportunity to be modest. Instead, she gave the impression that she was doing the local little-theatre group a great favor by playing the feminine leads in its shows. When she wasn't insisting that she belonged on Broadway, she was complaining to the long-suffering director that her parts didn't give her the acting scope she deserved.

When a promising newcomer joined the group, the director promptly gave her the lead in the next scheduled play. Mrs. Gavin's reaction was immediate and explosive. Cornering the director, she criticized his judgment, taste and mental ability. The new woman, she said, was not only dowdy-looking but also completely lacking in talent.

"While, as everyone knows," Mrs. Gavin said finally, "my own acting ability has never been questioned."

"Questioned?" the weary director exploded. "When has it ever been mentioned?"

—*U.F. Newlin*

Saving Face

Mrs. B___, a dowdy-looking woman with a penetrating voice, had bar__ 'joined the group of women around the cosmetics demon___ator in the big store when she started making critical __mm__ts. Starting with the outer row of spectators, she gradu__ly p__hed her way to the front, punctuating her passage with __sap__roving remarks. She explained to those nearest her why

Beat he Clock

she disliked beauty aids, what was wrong with the demonstrator's technique and how useless such cosmetics were to the women of today.

The demonstrator, maintaining a pleasant smile, ignored these all-too-audible comments until Mrs. Bains took advantage of a pause in her talk to announce, "I never use stuff like that."

The demonstrator gave Mrs. Bains a quick glance that took in her wedding ring. Then, in a pleasant voice, she observed to those around her, "His second wife will."

—*Katherine Laure*

Showing True Colors

The defense attorney was an expert at discrediting prosecution witnesses. His sarcastic questioning soon reduced them to quivering courtroom butts whose word no jury would accept. To break the state's case in an important trial, he fired questions unrelentingly at a mild little housewife who insisted that she could identify the car used in the crime.

"It was," she reiterated patiently, "a 194? medium gray with a flat finish and whitewall tires."

"You are so sure," the attorney sneered, "that I would like you to tell this jury—how long have you been studying the colors of 1949 models?"

The housewife replied, "Since 1949."

—*Pete P. erson*

Curve Ball

The man who could fix everything began to bluster the moment he heard that the local baseball club had invited 58 youngsters to be its guests at a doubleheader, but had limited the free adult attendance with them to three men.

"Why, that's ridiculous," he announced. "I know the manager. I know the president of the club. I'll straighten it out for you. With that many boys, there should be at least ten men along. I'll see that dad gets a break, too. Leave it to me."

Picking up the handiest phone, the man demanded first the president and then the manager of the club. The girl secretary who answered the phone insisted that neither was in.

"Now see here," the man asserted, "you can't brush me off like that. What you are doing for these boys is very generous, but you ought to do it right. You don't want these youngsters running wild all over the ball park, and you know good and well that no three men, myself included, can make 58 boys behave."

"Perhaps not," the girl replied, "but three women could."

—*Fisher Banks*

Book Ends

Sam, a power-drive type of book salesman, never opened a volume except to demonstrate the strength of its binding. But he talked so fast and continuously that he outsold salesmen with superior products.

Once, while showing a new textbook to a group of high-school principals, he noticed a rival salesman waiting at the rear of the room. As Sam knew little of the contents of his own book, he concentrated on boosting its durability. Banging the book on a table, he pointed out that no other product could be as sturdy. Opening the book, he bent the covers back until they met and then he stood on the book and jumped up and down.

As he bounced, Sam pointed a triumphant finger at the other salesman. "I'm willing to bet," he called out, "that your textbook won't stand a test like this."

"My book," the rival salesman answered quietly, "was made for the other end of the child."

—*A.M. Moseley*

Beat the Clock

Brushed Aside

The sour-faced, oddly dressed lady was poking among the brooms in the hardware store when a clerk asked if there was anything he could help her with.

"I doubt it!" she snapped. "Nothing here is worth buying." Then, picking up broom after broom, she discarded each with a short critical comment: "Flimsy! Cheap straw! Poor handle! Shoddy material!"

Seizing the last broom in the stock, she shook it under the nose of the bewildered clerk and said angrily, "Not like the brooms they used to make! Give the floor a good sweep with this one and it would fall apart! What's it good for?"

"Well," the clerk said, after a thoughtful pause, "you may find that it flies wonderfully."

—*Susan Cole*

Equal Time

The young comedian, who was almost as good as he thought he was, had ordered his five writers to meet him in a midtown restaurant to plan his next TV show. As usual, he ignored all their suggestions, complained at length that his genius was being wasted on poor lines and hinted that there were plenty of other writers around to be hired.

While the writers silently simmered, a friend of the comedian's stopped at the table. The comedian greeted him effusively, but instead of introducing the others by name, he just waved toward them and said, "These are my writers."

Soon afterward, a friend of one of the writers paused at the table. "Sit down, Hal, old man," the writer said warmly. "I'm sure you know all the writers here." He paused and waved toward the comedian. "But I'd like you to meet our actor."

—Andy Andrews

Phone Rites

Anyone who ever stuck his head in the small-town telephone exchange knew why it took so long to put through a call. It wasn't because the exchange was swamped, but because, through some prank of fate, the lone operator was also the town's most long-winded gossip. Being ideally located to collect and pass along back-fence news, she gabbed continually while unheeded calls lit up the switchboard like a Christmas tree. Local folks complained in vain. Nobody else wanted the confin-

Beat the Clock

ing job, so they had to put up with her.

All this was unknown to a stranger who tried to telephone from a local old-style hand phone equipped with crank and bell on the side to summon the operator. He cranked the bell several times. No answer. He cranked again. Still no answer. Exasperated, he cranked with a force which nearly tore the phone from the wall.

Then the voice of the operator interrupted sweetly, "Did you ring, sir?"

"Ring?" the stranger exploded. "Hell, no, I wasn't ringing! I was tolling—I thought you were dead!"

—*Neil Claire*

Trial and Error

Having lost a decision in a lower court, the young lawyer tried very hard to avoid any mistakes as he appealed the case in a higher court. He was especially careful to support each of his contentions with statutes and Supreme Court decisions.

The presiding judge, noted for his impatience with lawyers, viewed the young man's efforts with obvious boredom. He played with a pencil, gazed off into space and frequently shifted his position. After the lawyer read an important but lengthy decision in support of a point, the judge interrupted him.

"Young man," he snapped, "you may assume that this court knows the elementary principles of law!"

"Oh, I couldn't assume that, Your Honor," the lawyer protested politely. "That's the mistake I made in the lower court."

—*Bern J. Henry*

Watch Out

Jim prided himself on knowing all the shortcuts and easy ways through life. His favorite line began, "Why kill yourself working when——" Called into a conference with other salesmen, he heard the sales manager announce a new plan: With his monthly quota, each salesman would be given a wrist watch engraved with his name and the date. Thus, whenever he looked at the time, he would be reminded to strive to sell his quota.

The minute the meeting broke up, Jim let it be known that he wasn't going to respond to this spur. Thinking the sales manager was out of earshot, he announced with a broad grin, "After all, what can they do with a watch that already has a guy's name engraved on it?"

"Well," said the sales manager, who overheard the remark, "it would make him a nice going-away present."

—*Francis O. Walsh*

Taking the Lead

The cub reporter of a Midwestern daily was sweating over the annual "circus-comes-to-town" feature story. He had already turned in one version, which had been profanely rejected by the crusty city editor, a veteran of 30 years in this same newsroom.

Beat the Clock

And now, having submitted his second effort, the cub stood shivering while the city editor read it—and groaned aloud.

"Awful!" the editor rasped. "Terrible! You don't put any life or color in your writing. Where's your imagination? Take it away! Try again!"

Desperate, and embarrassed because fellow workers had been listening, the harried cub retreated to a far corner of the city room in search of inspiration. Back at his desk, he began pounding at his typewriter again. Once more he handed in his copy.

The city editor read the latest effort and slammed the copy down on his desk in disgust. "Worse and worse!" he roared. "Why, this lead alone would've got a man fired in my time."

"I can't agree with you, sir," the cub replied steadily and with surprising assurance.

"Oh, you can't, can't you?" the editor roared. "And may I ask what in hell makes you so sure?"

Turning, the cub pointed over to his desk, on which stood a faded bound file of many years earlier.

"Because I copied that lead, word for word, from the 1920 files," he said, "and the story has your by-line on it."

—Ed Hutchinson

Winning Ticket

George, who lived a fast life in the city, was driving through the small country town as if all speed laws suddenly had been repealed for his benefit.

"Don't worry," he soothed his concerned companion. "Out here I can buy my way out of any traffic trouble."

Soon afterward George was stopped by a rural policeman.

"Just watch how I handle this yokel," he said confidently. Then, taking his license from his wallet, George folded a five-dollar bill around it and handed both to the policeman.

Silently the officer returned the money and started writing out a ticket.

"Now look, officer," George protested. "Surely we can handle this thing in a friendly way."

"Certainly, sir." The officer didn't even look up. "I'll smile when I give you this ticket, and you smile when you accept it."

—Rada Ionesco

Your Ad

The high school tennis courts backed up to the grounds of the rectory of a very large and very "stylish" church. Occasionally, exuberant youngsters whammed a tennis ball over the fence and onto the trim lawns of the rectory—and, naturally, had to go after it.

The courts had been in use only a few weeks when a player, chasing after a stray ball, came face to face with a large sign on the rectory grounds, "No trespassing."

The "no trespassing" sign came down overnight, however, after the tennis club erected its own sign directly opposite. The sign read, "Forgive us our trespasses."

—*Jacqueline Lee*

Small Change

The lady was sublimely self-centered. She appeared only vaguely aware that anybody else existed on earth. So, during the rush hour at the post office, she asked for one three-cent stamp. Only after the clerk handed it to her did she take out her purse. While the line behind her lengthened, she got out one penny, then another. "I must have another somewhere," she remarked, and continued rummaging through her handbag.

Beat the Clock

Finally she looked up at the clerk and said reluctantly, "I suppose I'll have to give you a nickel."

"That's all right, madam," he replied. "I can break it for you."

—P.L. Elkins

Cut Rate

McJerkin, widely known as a man with one-way moneybags, happened to be in a business that flourished with every price rise. But that did not prevent him from howling constantly about the rising cost of living.

When haircuts at his favorite barbershop suddenly went up from one dollar to $1.25, he roared with anguish and went into a lengthy act. Pointing to his almost bald head, with its vague fringe of hair, he demanded a special reduced rate.

"How the devil," he ranted, "can you justify charging $1.25 to cut my hair?"

"Easy," the weary barber replied. "One dollar to look for the hair and 25 cents to cut it."

—Robert Y. Roberts

To Be Continued

Exuding confidence, the bright young medical student was making his first physical diagnosis. Most of his second-year classmates were nervous as they interviewed residents of an old folks' home whose growing ills had been diagnosed by a succession of medical classes through the years. But not this student.

Carefully deepening his voice to an impressive tone, he asked his subject, an elderly lady, to give him all her symptoms. He took them down in detail, mentally congratulating himself on his smooth bedside manner, then asked, "Now, are you sure you've named all your symptoms?"

"Oh, no," she said, "not all."

The student frowned. "Don't you realize that every symptom, no matter how slight, may be important? Now tell me just what you failed to mention."

"Well, I didn't mention my neuroses . . . for your sake," the old lady explained.

"For *my* sake?" the student asked irritably.

"Yes," said the old lady gently; "you see, you won't even get to study neuroses until next year."

—*Adelaide Strange*

Beat the Clock

Clerical Error

As he grew more sure of himself in his new pulpit, the young clergyman unfortunately became more long-winded. He also fancied himself increasingly as an interpreter of theological doctrine. So his sermons became lengthy, dry and theoretical. Often unable to follow him, many of those who were attracted to his services at the start ceased to attend. Summoning the deacons and lay leaders, the clergyman all but rebuked them for failing to see that the congregation attended services.

"I have given my best," he concluded. "I have spared no effort. As commanded in First Peter, Second Chapter, Second Verse, I have sought to nourish their souls with 'the sincere milk of the Word.' So what is wrong?"

"Perhaps," a deacon replied gently, "they prefer it condensed."

—F. W. Muse

Slow Burn

The young teachers'-college graduate, interviewed by a small-town school board, answered all questions patiently and politely. She explained why she wished to teach in a small school, what her philosophy of education was, and so on. She and the board appeared to be getting along nicely when a late arrival pitched in. He promptly began a personal inquisition.

"How many weekends a month do you expect to stay in town?" he demanded. "Are you available to sing in the church choir? . . . Do you have a steady boyfriend?"

Finally the man said, "As a member of this board, I would like to know whether you smoke."

"Not well enough, sir," she replied evenly, "to teach it."

—Frances Grier

Real Tear Jerker

Tom, a confident young attorney, was having a wonderful time telling a group of attentive law students what a high-flying legal eagle he was.

Having explained to them at great length just how he handled a judge and jury, Tom launched into a detailed description of his first jury trial.

"Somehow," he admitted, "I caught the sympathy of the jury. I had them right in the palm of my hand. Even the judge was impressed." Tom paused to greet an older lawyer, who had stopped beside the group, then added impressively, "You know, my father was in the courtroom that day, and by the time I finished there were tears in his eyes."

"Oh," the older lawyer said dryly, "was he a lawyer too?"

—*Richard L. Sullivan*

Play Acting

The community's Little Theater Guild was invaded one season by an overpowering young female who regarded herself as the logical leading lady in every guild play. Although she lacked talent, she insisted upon reading the top roles in tryouts. Turned down for the roles, she badgered the long-suffering director, and harassed board members with demands that they put pressure on the director to recognize her acting ability.

Forced by such tactics to give her another chance, the director permitted her to read the part of a sensitive, tragic young woman. She did it as though she were playing the town floozy.

Beat the Clock

At the end, she turned on the director and snapped: "And how would you like to see the part played?"

Gently he replied, "By an actress."

—*Vivian Garrigues*

Professional Advice

While standing in line for seats in a crowded Seattle restaurant, I overheard the young couple before me talking about buying baby clothes. As the waitress walked by with a tray, the young woman said to her husband, "My, that creamed chicken looks tempting."

The husband replied, "You know, dear, it isn't good for you or the baby to gain weight rapidly. You'd better have a salad."

At that, a stout middle-aged woman who had also overheard the conversation said to the wife, "Isn't that just like a man! They think they know everything. You take my advice and eat anything you want, whenever you want to, dearie. I always did, and I had four healthy children." Turning to the man, she asked triumphantly, "And just how many children have *you* brought into the world, young man——"

"One hundred and thirty-two as of yesterday, madam," he replied mildly. "I'm an obstetrician."

—*Elizabeth Steele*

Your Order, Please?

When the volunteer firemen rolled up to the burning bungalow, the owner, a short-spoken little woman, ran up to their red truck and made it very plain that she wanted her home saved, but strictly on her own terms.

"Don't trample my shrubs!" she shouted. "And stay out of my flower beds! And you there, put away that ax! Nobody is going to smash my windows or chop holes in my roof!"

The firemen had no sooner uncoiled their hose lines than the woman tangled with them, warning, "Be careful with that water! I don't want everything in the house soaked!"

When one of the volunteers lifted a heavy chemical extinguisher, she rushed at him and nearly bowled him over. "No chemicals on my furniture!" she screamed.

Setting down the extinguisher, the fireman asked, "And how would you like your home, madam, medium rare or well done?"

—G. Richard Larson

Body and Soul

The determined young clergyman and the obstinate old physician took directly opposing views. The clergyman, who had been admitted to the delivery room when his first child was born in another city, wished the same privilege for the arrival of his second. The physician would not hear of it. "But," said the clergyman, "my wife says it comforts and strengthens her for me to be close at hand."

The physician, blocking the door to the delivery room, replied snappishly, "As a preacher, you're a professional. So why

Beat the Clock

can't you understand another professional's viewpoint? Do you want people around when you're writing a sermon?"

"No," the clergyman agreed. "But I certainly do when I'm delivering one."

—*Mrs. Paul Gerrard Jackson*

Without Reservation

The harried railroad reservations clerk took a firm grip on the telephone and struggled to maintain his line's policy of courtesy under any circumstances. But the woman caller, already shrill and angry, persisted in demanding that space be found for her to go to Chicago the next morning.

She announced that any company which employed such uncooperative people deserved to be put out of business, that her husband had important connections who would not tolerate the treatment given her, and now, what was the clerk going to do about it?

"Madam," the clerk said politely, "as I explained, there is no space left. But if you will give me your name and telephone number, I'll be glad to notify you of any cancellation."

"Oh," the woman sputtered, "this is stupid!"

"Thank you," the clerk replied. "And your phone number?"

—*Marian Edwards*

Copy Editor

Mulcahey, a veteran *New York News* printer, has been around long enough to give the makeup editors pointers on handling news in type. If they dispute his suggestions in the rush of making a deadline, he roars good-humoredly at them, "You're driving me crazy!"

When Mul went on vacation, his place was taken by a young printer who admired him greatly and tried to imitate him in all respects. One day while working on a golf story, the novice made a suggestion which the sports makeup editor vetoed. Falling back on Mul's old standby, the youngster yelled, "You're driving me crazy!"

The editor looked him up and down and replied, "That's not a drive, son; that's a putt."

—*Bill Matthias*

Rebuttal

Harry C. Nixon, one of Ontario's most prominent Liberals and a perennial member of the Canadian House of Commons, was addressing a gathering consisting mostly of farmers.

These hardy sons of the soil were not in accord with the policies of Nixon's party, and he was being subjected to considerable heckling. One robust farmer spoke up: "Hey, Nixon! You call yourself a farmer, let's see the calluses on your hands."

Whereupon Nixon retorted, "My friend, before I came here tonight, I spent eight hours on a binder in a 30-acre field of oats. If you call *yourself* a farmer, you know the calluses are not on my hands."

—*William J.R. Bennett*

Skinflint

The self-made man persisted in sidetracking the minister's appeals for funds for church youth work with stories of his personal struggle for success.

The minister, sensing a complete refusal, arose to take his leave. "I only wish," he said, "that you could realize how much the boys and girls have been counting on you for support of their program."

"That's nice," the self-made man boomed, "but when I was growing up, I never had anybody to count on except myself. See those worry lines in my face? They're there because the only person I ever put faith in was myself. What do you think of that?" he asked.

"In that case," the minister replied with a smile, "don't you think it's time you had your faith lifted?"

—*Rex Raney*

Mental Note

The guest conductor of a symphony orchestra had not had much experience and he was anxious to make an impression upon the musicians. Happening to discover a misprint in the second-oboe part in one of the numbers he was about to rehearse, he said nothing about it until the orchestra passed the measure containing the error; then he rapped sharply on his music stand and, as the music stopped, said reprovingly, "In the twelfth bar of the allegro, the second oboe played a B flat. It should have been a B natural."

Observing that one of the men had hesitantly raised his hand, he asked impatiently, "Well, well, what is it?"

"Sir," said the musician, "the second oboe isn't here today."

—*Anna Woodruff*

Flooding the Lines

During a recent Missouri River flood, when telephone circuits in the disaster area were swamped with emergency calls, one woman was loudly irritable about the slowness of the service. Having reached a harried operator in Topeka and learned that her call to Southern Kansas would be delayed at least two hours, she launched into a lengthy criticism of the phone company and its operators.

"I'm calling relatives in the flood area," she said, "and I must talk to them immediately!"

Beat the Clock

"I'm sorry," the weary operator said. "I'll try later."

"But later won't do!" the lady snapped. "I want to find out how they are *now*! I'm worried."

"I'm worried, too," the operator gently answered. "I'm standing in two feet of water."

—*Mickey McDonald*

Hot Line

Rushing to cover a raging grain elevator fire near Toledo, reporter George Hewes found that the only phone booth available was in a next-door building which was, itself, about to go up in flames. While helpful firemen played their hoses around the booth, Hewes gamely began phoning in the story. He told how the fire started, who detected it, how it was being fought and what damage it had done.

The rewrite man on the other end of the line, far from being satisfied, began shooting questions. How tall was the grain elevator? How full was it? What color was it?

With flames almost licking the phone booth, Hewes shouted, "The firemen are ordering me out of here! I'll call you later!"

"Hold on," the rewrite man ordered. "I've got one more question: How soon are they going to rebuild?"

"Not," snapped Hewes, "until it cools."

—*Carter Townes*

Two's Company

The young business executive, assigned to special work which required a high degree of concentration, moved to a small and secluded rear office to carry out his task. To avoid unnecessary interruptions, he hung a small sign on the door, PLEASE KNOCK BEFORE ENTERING.

The office bore, a vice-president who was continually in search of something to do or someone to badger, barged through the door one day without knocking.

"What goes on back here?" he demanded. "Why do you have that silly sign on your door?"

"That sign is a reading test," the young executive replied evenly. "And you would be surprised at the people who fail it."

—*Mildred M. Flammer*

Old Doc, New Tricks

An older doctor in the community was known for his almost ruthless disregard of modern developments in medicine. He seldom bothered to read a medical journal, and used the same techniques that he had learned much earlier in medical school.

During one of his rare attendances at a medical meeting, he interrupted a younger doctor's discussion of a difficult and unusual case to say that the correct diagnosis was "obviously" just

Beat the Clock

the opposite of what the younger man had said.

When the young doctor replied that the laboratory reports eliminated that possible diagnosis, the older man thundered, "I don't care what the laboratory reports show; I have had 28 years of experience in the practice of medicine!"

"No, doctor," the younger man replied softly, "you have had one year's experience 28 times."

—J.L. Ewing, M.D.

Seeing Red

The big convertible shot through the red light and the traffic policeman whistled it to the curb. The driver was completely in the wrong, yet, as the policeman started to write out a ticket, he complained as bitterly as if he had been stopped while walking to church.

First he produced an array of cards from his wallet showing he was a member of various important organizations. Then he hinted darkly of high civic connections. Finally, when he saw that none of his arguments was having any effect, he glared at the policeman and rumbled, "You know, as a taxpayer, I'm the man who pays your salary!"

The officer paused in his writing just long enough to reply. "Then you'll be glad to know that I earn it."

—S.M. Diamond

Newsworthy

The special newsmen's plane, crammed with notables of the press, radio and television, was returning from an assignment. A young radio commentator with a brash, strident voice seized the opportunity to revel in his own importance. He boasted to the veteran newswriters and cameramen of his "vast audience," and, above all, of how quickly he could put across his news.

"Now you fellows couldn't do this, but I can——" he began time and again, following with some glowing account of his fast exclusive broadcasts.

When the plane alighted, he invited several newspaper reporters to "come to my station and I'll treat you to a new experience—I can run you through our latest broadcasting setup."

"Thanks," one of the reporters said crisply. "Come to our newspaper office and we'll gladly give you a new experience—we can run you through our press."

—*Lester B. Colby*

Suit Yourself

Into the men's clothing store came a large, loud woman meekly trailed by a subdued-looking man. The woman announced that she wanted a suit for her husband. She reeled off specifications, measurements and requirements. "And," she concluded, "I want to see only the suits that are in your special sale."

The clerk obediently shuffled through several racks of suits on

Beat the Clock

sale. He laid out five for inspection. One by one the woman rejected them. She then began scolding the clerk as if he were a small boy.

"Why, your prices are outlandish," she asserted. "I could have a suit made of that material for myself for one third of your bargain price."

"Tell me, ma'am," the clerk said politely, "would that be with one pair of pants or two?"

—*Joseph W. McKenney*

Show and Tell

Young Reverend Atwood greatly admired his own eloquence and power in the pulpit. So when he was assigned as assistant pastor of a large church, he gave his new congregation a full hour of it at every opportunity. After each lengthy sermon, he would hurry to the rear of the church to greet the parishioners and collect the congratulations he was so sure he deserved.

Following one especially long sermon on eternity, when compliments were very scarce, Atwood finally turned to the older clergyman whom he assisted. "Well," he said with quiet pride, "I really think I gave the congregation a thorough explanation of eternity this morning."

"Yes," the older man said with a faint smile, "and you demonstrated it pretty well too."

—*Glenn R. Bernhardt*

Starcastic Remarks

coolean

Strike One

On a rainy afternoon many seasons ago, a female baseball fan barged into the training camp hotel of the Philadelphia Athletics to obtain autographs. She announced her desire to Bullet Joe Bush, A's pitcher, who squired her about the lobby and introduced her to Eddie Collins, Jack Barry, Herb Pennock, Wally Schang, Frank Baker, Stuffy McInnis and other members of the then world's championship club.

The lady's autograph book was bulging with signatures by the time she was presented by Bush to Charles Albert (Chief) Bender, the A's far-famed Chippewa player.

"Not the great Indian pitcher?" asked the lady.

"The same, madam," Bender assured her.

"But," gushed the lady, "I always thought Indians wore feathers."

"We usually do, madam," replied Bender, "but, you see, this is the molting season."

—Charley Scully

Four-year Warranty

When Woodrow Wilson was president of Princeton University, his busy routine on opening day was suddenly disrupted by the appearance of an overdressed mother clutching her bewildered young freshman by the hand. Planting the boy in one chair and herself firmly in another, the woman proceeded to cross-examine the president concerning the intellectual background, moral atmosphere and general standing of Princeton. She knew nothing of the place, she said, because her father and grandfather attended Harvard. Her husband, a Princeton alumnus, wanted their son to follow in his footsteps, but, frankly, she had her doubts.

"William being our only child, we want him to have the very best of everything," she continued. "We want him to be absolutely outstanding in all his endeavors. We want him to receive an education which will mold him for greater things. Can you assure me that William will do well here?"

"Madam," Woodrow Wilson said mildly, "we guarantee satisfaction or we return the boy."

—*Calvin M. Floyd*

Starcastic Remarks

Spice of Life

A person of an extremely melancholy turn of mind was once pouring out his woes to Mark Twain.

The great humorist sat silently through outburst after outburst of pessimism. Finally the crapehanger, determined to make Twain quaver in his boots, leaned over and shouted into his impassive face, "Why, do you realize that every time I draw a mortal breath, an immortal soul passes into eternity?"

"Ever try cloves?" asked Mark.

—*Claire Cashen*

Degrees of Intelligence

Henry Ward Beecher never thought of himself as an intellectual; he always found men more absorbing than books, and he was aware that primarily it was his gift for oratory that made thousands flock to hear his sermons.

Once he was preaching in a small town where one of the local bigwigs had just been awarded a Ph.D. degree. This intellectual, while conversing with the famous preacher, remarked with little tact and much conceit, "Mr. Beecher, folks must wonder why it is that you don't have a Ph.D."

"Doctor," replied Mr. Beecher, "I'd rather have them wonder why I don't than why I do."

—*Frances Jones*

97

The Buck Stops Here

A lady with an almost over-powering knowledge of American wildlife of the outdoors kind beset Walt Disney at a dude ranch dinner at Palm Springs, California, after Disney's Bambi film was released.

With little ado, she proceeded to tell him in great detail what was wrong with the movie. Most of her criticism was that no deer would behave like the woodland creatures in Bambi.

"Why, in Bambi," she said, "the buck steps into the clearing ahead of the doe and fawn to be sure there are no hunters there. Actually, bucks hang back and have even been seen kicking the does out of the brush ahead of them. And the picture wasn't true to life in other respects, either."

"How right you are," Disney broke in gently. "And do you know something else wrong with it? Deer don't talk."

—*Elizabeth R. Miller*

Worse Verse

Miss Amy Lowell, the cigar-smoking poetess of the distinguished Boston family, was addressing the Poetry Society of South Carolina at Charleston in the days when DuBose Heyward and Hervey Allen were among its leading members. As the sole judge in awarding the society's important nation-wide poetry prize, Miss Lowell sought to explain why she selected a long and rambling offering in the then new and somewhat unintelligible style which she favored. "You must learn to appreciate it," she declared autocratically. Next, she read the poem, her choice of hundreds from all over the English-speaking world, to the perplexed and indignant audience.

At the end, most could mumble only pleasant inanities while shaking hands with the great lady. Then an elderly gentleman with a booming voice took her hand firmly, and said:

"To think, Miss Lowell, that there were 345 *worse* poems than that!"

—J. Mc.B. Wells

Primary Return

The late Alfred E. Smith, who fought his way up from the ranks politically, developed a knack for silencing even the most obnoxious hecklers with the fewest possible words. He did it so easily and pleasantly that only those around the stunned victims realized how hard they were hit.

At one large and important political gathering, however, the Happy Warrior seemingly chose to ignore a particularly loud and cantankerous heckler. Finally, this man took advantage of a pause between sentences to yell, "Go ahead, Al; tell 'em all you know! It won't take long!"

Smiling amiably at the man, Smith replied, "I'll tell them all we both know. It won't take any longer."

—Donald F. Burrows

The Royal Crown

Just about a hundred years ago, when Franz Liszt was called the Prince of Pianists, he gave a recital for the Czar of Russia. During the performance the Czar annoyed Liszt and the audience by talking constantly. For a time, Liszt ignored this irritating, impolite disturbance because of its source. But finally he lowered his hands from the keyboard and turned.

The audience waited in startled silence until the Czar demanded, "Why has the music stopped?"

"Sire," Liszt said gently, "when your Imperial Majesty speaks, the whole world is silent."

—*Margaret Chanler Aldrich*

The Long and Short of It

Having made up such stars as Bob Hope, Bing Crosby, George Raft and Dorothy Lamour, the little makeup man began to feel pretty big and important despite his bantam size. When his company went on location in Oklahoma, however, he was suddenly made size-conscious again by the rangy natives who gathered to watch the proceedings. After completing his makeup work early each day, he had time to lounge around, and this, of course, aroused the local curiosity. One day a six-

Starcastic Remarks

footer drawled, "Hey, Shorty, what's your job or ain't you big enough to have one?"

"My job," the makeup man replied loftily, "is to make up the actors. It takes intelligence, skill and artistry, not muscle." Eying the Oklahoman's brawny arms, he added, "I don't need muscles. All I ever have to lift is a powder puff."

Studying the little fellow, the big man asked, "What if there's powder on it?"

—Harry Ray

Getting to First Base

The sports editor of a New York daily, fed up with routine photographs, began urging the photographers to think up and make "pictures that are different."

One cameraman, duly goaded, decided to try some shots of a very tall Dodger first baseman demonstrating his tremendous reach. Knowing that managers are sometimes reluctant to permit their players to pose, he approached Leo Durocher.

Durocher mistrusted the proposal. The first baseman happened to be a rookie, and Durocher felt that the new man's picture in the paper might stir up jealousies.

When the photographer insisted, Durocher shouted, "What are you trying to do? Make a clown out of the guy?"

Drawing a deep breath, the photographer shouted back, "You don't expect me to make a first baseman out of him, do you?"

—Shirley Scott

Dead End

Woodrow Wilson, although accustomed to being besieged by office seekers, was particularly annoyed by one persistent politician. Finally the fellow played directly into his hands.

"Mr. President," he asked bluntly, "you remember the man you appointed to the Federal Trade Commission last week? Well, he died this morning. Would it be all right with you if I were to take his place?"

Wilson eyed the politician a moment, then nodded. "Certainly, if you can arrange it with the undertaker."

—Marie Forsberg

Enemy Lines

Just before the recent war, a Hollander found it necessary to take a business trip into Germany. He kept to himself and got along very well until he entered the diner of a German train. There a hulking waiter greeted him with the customary Nazi salute and "Heil Hitler!" When the man made no reply, the waiter reprimanded him sharply.

"I am a Hollander, and Hitler means nothing in Holland," the man retorted.

The waiter replied angrily, "Maybe not now. But someday you'll have our *Führer* in Holland too."

"Perhaps so," the Hollander chuckled. "We already have your Kaiser."

—O.E. Hinrichs

Poetic Justice

Local zeal in questioning literary celebrities during their one-night stands in small towns has caused many an author acute anguish. Not all of them manage to emerge as unscathed and unperturbed as Carl Sandburg did at a campus tea at the State Teachers College at Indiana, Pennsylvania, some years ago.

During a lull in the conversation, the faculty members and others present were horrified to hear an assured young first-year student accost the famous poet and ask pertly:

Starcastic Remarks

"Mr. Sandburg, do you consider yourself a success?"

Drawing himself up with quiet dignity, he replied sonorously, "Young woman, do you realize that you are addressing the chairman of the board and president of the North American Pawpaw Growers' Association?"

—*Carrie Belle Parks*

By George

While serving as secretary of defense, General George C. Marshall was harried by a reporter who asked long, misleading questions in an obvious effort to trick him into making some imprudent statement. Patiently, the general would sift the facts from these confusing queries and answer as best he could. This simply encouraged the reporter to ask more involved questions.

Finally, after he had completed one of his longest and trickiest queries, General Marshall gave him a weary smile.

"Would you mind," he said pleasantly, "repeating what you just tried to say?"

—*R.F. Karolevitz*

The Tennis Racket

When I was 18, I managed to reach the quarter-finals in the national junior indoor tennis championships. There I was matched against Vincent Richards, still a junior but already one of the world's leading tennis players. Beating him was out of the question, of course. The most I hoped for was to take four games, because my father had promised me a new racket if I did.

Richards blanked me in the first set, 6—0. Coming back furiously, I took my four games in the second set before going down, 6—4. That not only earned me my racket but represented more games than anyone else had taken from the great Richards during the tournament. By letting my mind dwell on that fact far into the night, I eventually convinced myself that the boy wonder of tennis had narrowly escaped defeat. I visualized big headlines on the sports pages next morning: "Cummings Hands Richards Near-Upset" or perhaps "New Star Looms on Tennis Horizon."

Bright and early, I rushed for the papers. Sure enough, the first one I picked up *did* headline my match with Richards. It read: RICHARDS WAY OFF FORM IN JUNIOR TOURNEY.

—*Parke Cummings*

Starcastic Remarks

Defensive End

Long after the sensational 1925 Rose Bowl game between Notre Dame, with its famous "Four Horsemen," and an equally great Stanford team sparked by the fabulous fullback, Ernie Nevers, controversy raged over whether Nevers had scored on a line plunge. The officials and the scoreboard said he didn't, and Notre Dame won.

At one of the periodic revivals of the argument years later at a gathering of sports writers and football celebrities, a noisy West Coast sports scribe stated positively that Nevers made a touchdown. Outtalking all opposition, this man proclaimed: "I had an unobstructed view from the press box and held my glasses on Nevers throughout the play. I say he scored."

"I say otherwise," a quiet man spoke out from the background.

"Just who are you, and where were you sitting?" the sports writer challenged.

"My name is Harry Stuhldreher, of Notre Dame," came the reply, "and I was sitting on Ernie Nevers."

—*Frank C. Winslow*